IN THE MIDST OF THE STORM: STILLNESS

*Be still, and know that I am God. I
will be exalted among the nations, I
will be exalted in the earth!
Psalm 46:10*

In the Midst of the Storm: Stillness

By

Paul L Cox
Barbara Kain Parker

IN THE MIDST OF THE STORM: STILLNESS

By Paul L Cox & Barbara Kain Parker

Aslan's Place Publications
9315 Sagebrush Street
Apple Valley, CA 92308
760-810-0990
aslansplace.com

All Rights Reserved. No part of this book may be reproduced or transmitted in any form or by any means—electronic or mechanical, including photocopying, recording, or by any information storage and retrieval system—without written permission from the authors except as provided by the copyright laws of the United States of America. Unauthorized reproduction is a violation of both federal and spiritual laws.

Unless otherwise indicated, scriptures are taken from the The ESV® Bible (The Holy Bible, English Standard Version®) copyright © 2001 by Crossway Bible, a publishing ministry of Good News Publishers. Used by permission. All rights reserved.

Other Biblical references:

New King James Version (NKJV): New King James Version®. Copyright © 1982 by Thomas Nelson, Inc., publishers. Used by permission. All rights reserved.

Scripture quotations marked NLT are taken from the *Holy Bible*, New Living Translation, copyright ©1996, 2004, 2015 by Tyndale House Foundation. Used by permission of Tyndale House Publishers, Inc., Carol Stream, Illinois 60188. All rights reserved.

Copyright 2023, by Paul L Cox & Barbara Kain Parker

All rights reserved.

Cover Design: Brodie Schmidtke

ISBN: 979-8-3996-8475-8

Printed in the United States of America

Dedication

In the Midst of the Storm, Stillness is dedicated to the One who made everything possible:

> *In the beginning was the Word, and the Word was with God, and the Word was God. He was in the beginning with God. All things were made through Him, and without Him nothing was made that was made. In Him was life, and the life was the light of men. And the light shines in the darkness, and the darkness did not comprehend it.*[1]

> *In him you also, when you heard the word of truth, the gospel of your salvation, and believed in him, were sealed with the promised Holy Spirit… that the God of our Lord Jesus Christ, the Father of glory, may give you the Spirit of wisdom and of revelation in the knowledge of him, having the eyes of your hearts enlightened, that you may know what is the hope to which he has called you, what are the riches of his glorious inheritance in the saints, and what is the immeasurable greatness of his power toward us who believe, according to the working of his great might that he worked in Christ when he raised him from the dead and seated him at his right hand in the heavenly places, far above all rule and authority and power and dominion, and above every name that is named, not only in this age but also in the one to come.*[2]

Adoni, YHVH (Yahweh), I Am, the Lord
Abba, the Father
Yeshua HaMashiach, Jesus the Messiah, the Son of God
Ruach ha-Kodesch, the Holy Spirit

[1] John 1:1-4

[2] Ephesians 1:13, 17-21

Table of Contents

ENDORSEMENT 9

PROPHETIC WORDS 11

PREFACE 13

INTRODUCTION 15

CHAPTER ONE: *NO ONE EVER TOLD ME…* 17

CHAPTER TWO: *WHAT? I HAVE TO DIE???* 38

CHAPTER THREE: *COUNTING THE COST* 47

CHAPTER FOUR *GOD'S WAITING ROOM* 54

CHAPTER FIVE: *CARS & FAITH* 62

CHAPTER SIX: *DEFINING FAITH* 68

CHAPTER SEVEN: *ENDURING FAITH* 76

CHAPTER EIGHT: *A HOPE THAT ENDURES* 85

CHAPTER NINE: *ENTERING THE REST* 93

CHAPTER TEN: *KNOWING GOD* 113

CHAPTER ELEVEN: *ENCOUNTERING STILLNESS* 121

CHAPTER TWELVE: *STILLNESS ABSOLUTES* 131

CHAPTER THIRTEEN: *HOLINESS AND THE EXPLOSIVE POWER OF GOD'S HEART* 139

CONCLUSION 156

Endorsement

On August 7, 1990, President George Herbert Walker Bush organized Operation Desert Shield in response to Iraq's invasion of Kuwait on August 2nd. Prior to the invasion, President Bush vehemently maintained that Saddam Hussein had accumulated a large stockpile of WMD's (Weapons of Mass Destruction). After a lengthy search and much to President Bush's disappointment, no WMD's were found.

As a pastor for over 30 years, I have interacted with and ministered to hundreds of people who have been affected by different types of WMD's, hell-sent hindrances that have included, but not limited to, adversity, discouragement, 'friendly-fire' criticism, debilitating health issues and financial lack, to name just a few. Although different, each of these demonic assignments or fiery darts from the enemy, are launched to persuade us to quit the race set before us by the Lord.

Unfortunately, WMD's are a part of our walk with God, but if we exercise persistent faith in the midst of each storm and abide in Christ, we will breakthrough time and again. Corrie Ten Boom wisely said, "Faith is like radar that sees through the fog - the reality of things at a distance that the human eye cannot see." *In the Midst of the Storm* is a book about persistent, patient faith that will help you 'see through the fog' while you are being barraged by enemy WMD's. It is a practical book that will teach you how to be at peace during the panic moments of your life and maintain your serenity while in the storm.

Bravo, Paul and Barbara, for writing a much-needed book that all can benefit from because of the challenging times in which we live today!

Rob Gross
Senior Pastor, Mountain View Community Church
Aiea, Hawaii
mvcchawaii.org

Prophetic Words

Draw near to Me in this venture for My ability; for you are on the verge of a new discovery, a new unexplored horizon of my love. Do not be afraid although the venture may seem daunting; I AM will lead you, guide you, and create the path before you. You are leaning into new levels and layers of trust. This is new experience of revelation that will guide and inform all who follow.

There is a practical application of truth that must be done; there is a practical application of my word that must be lived out in your lives. Each of you have been given a specific word and a specific truth since childhood that I have called thee to bear throughout your life. These pieces of Myself that I have given and placed in each of thee must be put together and assembled in your lives as you live out the truth of them.

Each of you sets each other up. As you each have been called to be faithful and mine the gold in my words, faith will explode on the earth. You are leading the way; you are living the way to the revival of hearts and minds; and the preparation of the lands, the homes, the hearts, the souls and the spirits of all those I have called into The Family.

Briana Lassiter
Sarasota , Florida

Who would call you to Rest?

Who would call you to Rest while the storms of life are bombarding you?

Who would call you to peacefully Rest while the waves are rocking your boat?

Who would do this?

What is His name?

How does He relate to you?

He is the Son of God Almighty

The one, true living God

Who holds all things together

Who gave his sinless life for you everywhere

And Jesus is his name.

Matt. 8:23-27:

> *And when he got into the boat, his disciples followed him. And behold, there arose a great storm on the sea, so that the boat was being swamped by the waves; but he was asleep. And they went and woke him, saying, "Save us, Lord; we are perishing." And he said to them, "Why are you afraid, O you of little faith?" Then he rose and rebuked the winds and the sea, and there was a great calm. And the men marveled, saying, "What sort of man is this, that even winds and sea obey him?"* [1]

Persis Tiner
Prayer Minister, Prophetic Intercessor
Los Angeles, California

---

[1] Matthew 8:23-27

PREFACE

Every book we have written together has been very much a collaborative effort in which the Lord has fused together our very-different spiritual gifts to produce cohesive messages. *In the Midst of the Storm, Stillness* is no exception; it could only be written by the grace of God, and we are grateful that He has chosen to use us to deliver this particular message.

When two or more people co-author a book, it can be confusing who is speaking at any given time, so we'd like to clarify up front who's who. Anything that is written in a first-person singular style (I, me, my) refers to Barbara; anything that originated with Paul is clearly identified with his name; and our shared thoughts will be indicated by 'we' or 'our'.

Looking back, we are astounded to realize that this is the eleventh book we've written together! What a blessed journey it has been, as we have attempted not only to do but also to only write about what the Father is placing before us. Through it we have truly enjoyed the blessings of unity:

> *For as in one body we have many members, and the members do not all have the same function, so we, though many, are one body in Christ, and individually members one of another. Having gifts that differ according to the grace given to us, let us use them...*[1]

> *Behold, how good and pleasant it is when brothers dwell in unity!* [2]

It should be noted that we never publish anything containing new revelatory insights or words from the Lord that hasn't already been tested among wise, trusted friends.

This is because we take very seriously the wisdom of the biblical proverbs:

Where there is no guidance, a people falls, but in an abundance of counselors there is safety.[3]

The way of a fool is right in his own eyes, but a wise man listens to advice.[4]

Without counsel plans fail, but with many advisers they succeed.[5]

...for by wise guidance you can wage your war, and in abundance of counselors there is victory.[6]

Our prayer for this book is that you will learn to encounter the peace and rest of His stillness in the midst of your personal storms of life.

Paul L Cox

Barbara Kain Parker

---

[1] Romans 12:4-6a

[2] Psalm 133:1

[3] Proverbs 11:14

[4] Proverbs 12:15

[5] Proverbs 15:22

[6] Proverbs 24:6

INTRODUCTION

In April 2023, neither of us thought we had any more books left in us, but then God started shaking things up.

First, there was a sermon that Paul preached in Aiea Hawaii at Mountain View Community Church. I thought it was the best sermon I've ever heard him preach, and that message is shared in the first chapter. Then, the Lord began speaking to me about stillness, and it escalated from there. When I first shared my notes regarding stillness with Paul, he responded, "I had a thought. My sermon on perseverance may be relevant for this. It is in the place of stillness that you can persevere. It is the stillness in the eye of the storm." Thus, our title, *In the Midst of the Storm, Stillness.*

Next the Lord began bringing more and more topics to mind that seemingly needed to be addressed; most of which we've spoken of often over the years but, surprisingly, have never discussed in one of our books except in passing.

The content has grown quickly from Paul's one sermon and my thoughts about stillness into a whole book full of long-overdue revelatory insights from the Lord, which we sense are necessary for the equipping of the Church for God's harvest season.

As has often been the case, this Introduction is one of the last things to be written. Perhaps that's because we usually don't have any idea what the Lord will inspire us to include when we begin. He's the One who inspires and develops everything we write. After all, how can anyone write an Introduction when there is no knowledge of what a book will be about?

This morning, the Lord shared from the life of Jesus what the point of the whole book is to be. The story is familiar:

> *On that day, when evening had come, he said to them, "Let us go across to the other side." And leaving the crowd, they took him with them in the boat, just as he was. And other boats were with him. And a great windstorm arose, and the waves were breaking into the boat, so that the boat was already filling. But he was in the stern, asleep on the cushion. And they woke him and said to him, "Teacher, do you not care that we are perishing?" And he awoke and rebuked the wind and said to the sea, "Peace! Be still!" And the wind ceased, and there was a great calm. He said to them, "Why are you so afraid? Have you still no faith?" And they were filled with great fear and said to one another, "Who then is this, that even the wind and the sea obey him?"*[1]

Like Jesus; disciples, we only see the storms, and we fear that we will be swept away by them; but just as Jesus spoke to the storm, "Peace be still," so He speaks to each of us as the trials of life hit us with hurricane force, "Peace, be still; know that I am God; for I am able to do far more abundantly than all that you can ask or think." [2]

---

[1] Mark 4:35-41

[2] Mark 4: , Psalm 46:10, Ephesians 3:20

CHAPTER ONE:
NO ONE EVER TOLD ME...

Note: This chapter is taken from a sermon that Paul preached at Mountain View Community Church in Aiea, Hawaii on Palm Sunday, 2023.

In 1980, when I was thirty- six years old, Donna and I got in a car with our three children and left Buell, Idaho to come to Bethel Baptist Church in Montclair, California. What a journey that trip started, which brings us to here and now; but let me go back to the beginning.

I was saved at the First Baptist Church of Honolulu, Hawaii at the age of six. My dad was in the Marine Corp and somewhere around 1952 we moved to the mainland. Eventually, I finished high school went to Pepperdine University; and during 1966, the year I graduated, my parents began attending the First Baptist Church of Downey, California. They said I needed to come there, but my sister and I were in a rebellious stage where we did not want to be going to church anywhere that our parents were attending. But, they finally convinced me, and I still remember that first Sunday night in the two-thousand-member church with a sanctuary that seated a thousand people. I had never heard anything like the choir backed by a full pipe organ and piano. It was just astonishing! This is also the first time I'd ever heard expository preaching, and I was hooked, as a pastor would preach through books of a Bible. At the time, we did not know that this was the beginning of the Jesus Movement.

One day I noticed a young lady Donna Mc Ilvaine - I espied her, watched her, and eventually we ended up teaching in the sixth-grade department. She had just finished high school and was eighteen years old, while I'd already finished college, but that was all right and we fell in love and got married. I taught history, English and reading for three years in a public school, and at the same time we began working as sponsors in the junior-high department. After a couple of youth pastors had come and gone, we were asked to take over the junior high department, which we did, and it grew to about a hundred students. Meanwhile, I was still teaching full time and I finally got to the point that I told the pastor I could either quit my job or resign from the youth department because I couldn't do both. As a result, we became full time youth pastors in 1971, and it was wonderful. Hundreds of kids came through that church, people were being saved daily, and it was the most extraordinary time; regardless of the fact that this was when we believed in the Father, the Son and the Holy Bible with no awareness of the presence and power of the Holy Spirit.

I've often compared this time in our lives to living in Camelot; while at this church we'd married, had three kids, watched the explosion of the youth ministry, and our lives were just amazing. I found out later, however, that the pastor was taking all the heat for us, and that I understood nothing about church drama because no one ever told me what the Christian life is really about.

I started having an impression that I was to speak; but I did not want to speak so I told the Lord, "I'm not going to do this." Now, keep in mind that these were the days before we even knew the Lord talks to us! But He kept convicting me that I should speak, and I kept arguing because I really didn't want to do it; so I tried bargaining and told Him, "If You want me to speak, then You'll have to cause something to happen." So the next day I got a call to speak at a camp;

and so the Lord took care of that! Then after I'd been doing that that for a while, the Lord told me He wanted me to become a pastor. But we were really happy at this time; as youth pastors we had about sixty leaders under us; we managed the junior high department, the children's department and I was teaching in the college department; we had an intern program, and I was just as happy as can be. I did not want to become a pastor! Then I became one, and quickly realized why I didn't want that. Again, no one had told me what the Christian life was really like.

We moved to Buell, Idaho, staying there for three winters, and I had my boot camp. I can honestly say that I was never depressed for even a day in my life until I became a pastor and started hearing people's problems. Donna and I had both grown up in Christian homes, our parents were good friends, we had the idyllic family and it was just wonderful. So, dealing with the traumas in other families was a huge stretch, and it didn't take long after becoming a pastor to begin thinking, "There has to be more than this."

In 1980, we received the call to a church back in Montclair, California on Easter Sunday. We left in a snowstorm and returned to Southern CA. Our new church had a sanctuary that sat five hundred people; we had a church staff and a bus; and the change was exciting and wonderful. I dug in, filled with energy and working; Donna now had a shopping center so she was happy; we were raising our children, and life was full; but little did we know what lay ahead.

In our first December back home in CA, I went to the pharmacy to pick up a prescription. That night, we were to go out to dinner with a missionary family from New Guinea that our church supported. We were meeting them for the first time, and I told Donna we were to go out to dinner so I told Donna I'd stop at the pharmacy on my way home. Standing at the counter, I suddenly felt something poking my back, so I turned around, and there was a man in a mask who'd stuck a gun in my back. He said, "This is a hold up and you've walked right into it; and I guess you haven't been part of a hold up before." I replied, "No, I haven't." He took me around the counter into the back where the pills were and had me get down on my knees. As he taped my hands behind my back, the only thought I had was that this was really going to ruin Donna's Christmas. I just knew I was going to be shot and I had the funniest feeling and thought, "I'm going to Heaven and it's going to be okay." You never know until you're in a crisis situation what something like that is really going to be like! There were two or three robbers, and fortunately they didn't shoot me, or anyone else for that matter. Finally, they left and the police came; we were all untied and the police starting asking questions. I was a mess, and when I tell you that you do not want to look at the robbers because you don't want them to think that you know who they are. I went home and Donna said, "Why are you so late?" I answered, "I guess you could say I was held up."

That began a series of things that happened in Montclair. Sometime later, I did a funeral for a man who had been divorced. Now, when you do a funeral you do not mention the divorced people - that's just not what you do - you mention the relatives, but not the ex. All seemed to be going well until this one lady seemed to be really mad at me , and it turned out she was the ex-wife. Then I got a call on a Saturday evening from someone asking what time the church service was. Now, I did not know about words of knowledge then; I was a Baptist after all, but I had this thought that the call was from that angry lady. The next morning, I preached my sermon and at the end of the service I saw her walking through the back door and knew she was after me. It was no surprise when the ushers came and told me I needed to talk with her, so I called all the biggest men in the church to the front at the end of the service we slowly walked out as a group. She started cursing at me and throwing things, and as she was leaving hit a kid and knocked a table over. Then in her car, she was driving back and forth lot, cursing and telling me what a terrible person I was. Meanwhile, I was thinking, "I'm just this nice Baptist pastor; what is my problem?"

So another time at a deacons' meeting, a friend called and said, "I don't want you to worry but all the Montclair police are at your house." What? Of course I'm not going to be worried about that at all! So I went home and sure enough, of all the police were there with lights flashing; so I asked what was going on, only to be told that someone who had just murdered someone in Pomona had fled and was now cornered inside the new addition we were adding onto our home; but everything should be OK because they had an officer armed with a shotgun guarding my family in the hallway.

Again, what was going on? I was just this nice Baptist pastor, a little guy who was just going along, dealing with the ordinary church stuff, the staff infections and people complaining; but then began noticing that every Sunday I would be absolutely exhausted by the time I finished preaching. There had been no exhaustion in either Idaho or at Downey First Baptist, and there was none when I preached elsewhere, but it was so bad here that I was drinking power drinks before going to church and between each service. Then my friend said that though he really liked my sermons, sometimes it was like all of my words were just falling to the ground. You see, no one ever told me what the Christian life was really about.

I thought everybody goes through all the stuff; then we die, and go to heaven. That was the extent of my understanding to the resistance that we face in our Christian life. But I noticed a pattern. We would have deacons and were governed by a deacon board; but I would actually tell the deacons up front that before they came on the board to understand that things might get really tough for them. I'd started figuring that out because as I watched people come into leadership and then, over and over again things would get really, really difficult; and I realized that there was something going on that I did not understand because no one ever told me what the Christian life is really all about.

I thought Christianity was just supposed to be wonderful and lovely; you'd come to church that it would be; exciting and wonderful. And then you'd go home and live a normal life in your marriage and with your family, and ours was wonderful but there's all the usual everyday drama, but that's just what life is like. Right?

We had all the drama that took place at that church, and eventually we left and went to another church with even more drama; left again and because I'd had a dream of actually being in the high desert, we moved there. We had been given enough money to live on for about six months, and I transitioned from full time to part time pastoring. Throughout all of this time, things became progressively worse, but the Lord had been teaching me how to pray for people to be free from oppression. He wouldn't stop, and as He just kept teaching me more and more, the resistance also grew more and more. Finally, I had to go back to teaching part time while still pastoring part time, but things kept going from bad to worse.

Finally, it got so hard that I realized the church I was pastoring was not going to make it because every time the power of God came more people left. Instead of a church that was growing, people were leaving; so we left too, and Donna and I had a discussion because I realized that my life was falling apart and I didn't know what we were going to do, so the default thing was to go back to teaching. Throughout this whole time, I continued praying for people, my discernment had been active for a couple of years and it kept growing; but by now we had lost probably three address books full of friends. People would just bail on us because the more the Power would come on me, and the more that I felt evil coming off of people, the more friends we lost. You see, no one ever told me what the Christian life is really about.

Donna and I sat together and tried to figure out what to do next, and I knew I needed to try to find a job. I was painting rooms and helping grade term papers; doing anything I could to make money. But I need to praise the Lord here because we never had an empty back account. I wondered what was going on because nothing was working, and I remembered that just before we left the Montclair church the associate pastor came to me and asked, "Have you ever thought that maybe you are the problem?" I thought, "I don't think that's quite true, but something is the problem." So Donna and I we sitting on the bed, when I had this thought, "You don't know if you're wrong if you stop." Okay; but you see, no one ever told me what the Christian life was really like.

What we heard from the pulpit was that it was all wonderful; but that's not what the Bible says, and the thought remains that we really do not know if we're wrong if we ever stop.

You know I love Hawaii and I love this church, and Pastor Rob is a good friend; but I've got through some difficult experiences over the last few years. When came the last time, I did not want to be here; I just wanted to go home, and every day I'd think, " I can't take this anymore." I did not understand what my problem was; I only knew I just wanted to go home.

This trip, we arrived on March 1, 2022, and Rob picked us up at the airport. I had discerned something territorially over Oahu that I'd never discerned before, so I asked Rob to pray, and the most amazing thing happened to me! The feeling of not wanting to be here absolutely disappeared. So you see, I was not the problem; the resistance was the problem, and another friend was experiencing the same thing. That is how much resistance there was; and you see, no one really told us what the Christian life was really about.

So what is it about? It's about persevering; it's about enduring; it's about not giving up; it's about continuing on in faith. It's not about running and going somewhere else; it's not saying that I'm done with this. That's what the Christian life is really about. You see, just as we love the honeymoon period of our marriage, we come home and then real life begins. We also love the honeymoon period of our Christian walk, because it's true that we fall in love with someone who is in love with us, and Jesus enters into our life as Savior, gives us His purpose and hope and joy, and it is just so wonderful; but then everyday life resumes and we start learning that there's resistance for some reason we cannot identify. We try to say well it must be that it's the pastor, so maybe if I just find a better pastor. Or maybe it's the people in the church ,or the leadership, or, or, or; and on it goes, as we bounce around trying to find answers; trying to find a way to get that honeymoon feeling back again instead of digging in and saying, "I am in this for the long haul, and I am not ever going to give up."

Paul knew this; the Apostle Paul is very honest about what the Christian life is. Remember, he's the one who talks about joy – Philippians is the book of joy – so let's look at some passages that tell us what the Christian life is really like:

> *Therefore, my beloved brothers, be steadfast, immovable, always abounding in the work of the Lord, knowing that in the Lord your labor is not in vain.*[1]

Well, if you're just sailing along, listening to feel-good sermons, you don't have to worry not the work of being steadfast, or immovable or laboring, do you?.

> *…but as servants of God we commend ourselves in every way: by great endurance, in afflictions, hardships, calamities, beatings, imprisonments, riots, labors, sleepless nights, hunger; beatings, imprisonments, riots, labors, sleepless nights, hunger; by purity, knowledge, patience, kindness, the Holy Spirit, genuine love; by truthful speech, and the power of God; with the weapons of righteousness for the right hand and for the left; through honor and dishonor, through slander and praise. We are treated as impostors, and yet are true; as unknown, and yet well known; as dying, and behold, we live; as punished, and yet not killed; as sorrowful, yet always rejoicing; as poor, yet making many rich; as having nothing, yet possessing everything.* [2]

I've had so many times in the last years that sometimes I don't sleep for a week until there's some sort of spiritual breakthrough, and I absolutely hate it; I do not like that part of my job. And fasting, uggg! On down the list, we all like the good stuff and we'll take the honor and praise parts; but no thanks to the dishonor, slander, sorrow or being poor; and just forget the dying part too!

When we moved to the high desert we lost our house, and by the time we moved to the mountains to start on the bottom and begin ministry again, we were down to the dining room set. We had lost everything else. No one told me about that part. Let's look at another passage:

> *Therefore, beloved, since you are waiting for these, be diligent to be found by him without spot or blemish, and at peace. And count the patience of our Lord as salvation, just as our beloved brother Paul also wrote to you according to the wisdom given him,*

Be diligent. That means make haste, zealous, showing great energy or enthusiasm in pursuit of a cause or objective. We are to be diligent; we are not to give up; we are to continue.

You're familiar with Hebrews 10-12, especially chapter 11, which we know as the faith chapter; but I want to suggest to you that these may be viewed as the endurance chapters:

> *But recall the former days when, after you were enlightened, you endured a hard struggle with sufferings, sometimes being publicly exposed to reproach and affliction, and sometimes being partners with those so treated. For you had compassion on those in prison, and you joyfully accepted the plundering of your property, since you knew that you yourselves had a better possession and an abiding one. Therefore do not throw away your confidence, which has a great reward. For you*

have need of endurance, so that when you have done the will of God you may receive what is promised.[3]

Then Chapter 11 begins, and all these people who operated by faith are listed. Verses 5-7:

> *By faith Enoch was taken up so that he should not see death, and he was not found, because God had taken him. Now before he was taken he was commended as having pleased God. And without faith it is impossible to please him, for whoever would draw near to God must believe that he exists and that he rewards those who seek him. By faith Noah, being warned by God concerning events as yet unseen, in reverent fear constructed an ark for the saving of his household. By this he condemned the world and became an heir of the righteousness that comes by faith.*

I looked up how long it took Noah to build the ark, and it was probably fifty-five to seventy-five years. Now think about how old you are. I want us to emotionally feel what it was like for Noah. Fifty-five to seventy-five years, he was enduring by faith. Then we move down to Abraham in the next verse:

> *By faith Abraham obeyed when he was called to go out to a place that he was to receive as an inheritance. And he went out, not knowing where he was going. By faith he went to live in the land of promise, as in a foreign land, living in tents with Isaac and Jacob, heirs with him of the same promise. For he was looking forward to the city that has foundations, whose designer and builder is God.*

I wondered how old Abraham was when he was called by God. Probably seventy-five years old, at which point we know he didn't have a child yet, the Lord said He'd make of him a great nation. No children yet, he's seventy-five years old, but he's called to leave everything behind and move to a new land. Then he has Isaac at a hundred and Sarah, his wife, laughs at the angels who brought the promise because after all, how likely was that?

Then, when Isaac was thirty-three, the same age that Jesus was when He went to the cross, Abraham was told by the Lord to go and sacrifice his son at the exact spot where God's son would eventually be crucified on Mt. Moriah. Of course, the didn't let Abraham go through with it, but He needed so see if he would be obedient.

Think of this; you have two obedient people here. The elderly Abraham; and Isaac, a grown man who is willing to be tied down by his father and sacrificed. So we go on to verse 22:

> *By faith Joseph, at the end of his life, made mention of the exodus of the Israelites and gave directions concerning his bones.*

Joseph was probably seventeen when he was sold into slavery and thirty when he was made co-regent of Egypt. That's a lot of years to endure, especially considering that he spent at least two or three years in jail, but did he give up? No. He persevered by faith, because he'd been given a promise of what was going to happen; and of course, that promise was fulfilled. Moving on:

> *Therefore, since we are surrounded by so great a cloud of witnesses, let us also lay aside every weight, and sin which clings so closely, and let us run with endurance the race that is set before us, looking to Jesus, the founder and perfecter of our faith, who for the joy that was set before him endured the cross, despising the shame, and is seated at the right hand of the throne of God.*[4]

On Palm Sunday we remember the day on which our Lord Jesus Christ as the God-man sat on a donkey as He entered Jerusalem. That was a clear sign to everybody present, because only a king would come into a country on a donkey, so everybody would have understood that Jesus was proclaiming His kingship. But a few short days later there was the Lord's Supper, and early on Friday morning the journey to the cross began.

> *For to this you have been called, because Christ also suffered for you, leaving you an example, so that you might follow in his steps.* [5]

It was because of the joy set before Him that he endured and suffered for us, showing through His personal example that we would follow in His footsteps. His steps are steps of coming against all the resistance as we follow Jesus; we do not stop; we do not give up. Oh, how I wanted to give up so many times; I am no saint in this and there are times when I cannot imagine how I can do this anymore; I'm so exhausted, so tired, and I wonder how I can get out of this assignment. Believe me, I'm no hero here but I don't know if I'm wrong if I stop; and what other choice is there? If you've tasted of Him, where else are you're going to go?

Apostle Paul wrote to the Corinthians:

> *Truly the signs of an apostle were accomplished among you with all perseverance, in signs and wonders and mighty deeds For what is it in which you were inferior to other churches, except that I myself was not burdensome to you? Forgive me this wrong!* [6]

It's not because everyone likes you, and are happy because they love your preaching. Rather, the sign of the apostle is *with all perseverance*, and willing to be less and inferior. So, to get to this point you have to be a nobody, first of all; and you need to overcome in battle.

On October 29, 1941, Winston Churchill gave a speech to Harrow School, his alma mater. He said this, in the throes of World War II:

> Never give in. Never give in. Never, never, never — in nothing, great or small, large or petty — never give in, except to convictions of honour and good sense. Never yield to force. Never yield to the apparently overwhelming might of the enemy.
>
> We stood all alone a year ago, and to many countries it seemed that our account was closed, we were finished. All this tradition of ours, our songs, our School history, this part of the history of this country, were gone and finished and liquidated.
>
> Very different is the mood today. Britain, other nations thought, had drawn a sponge across her slate. But instead our country stood in the gap. There was no flinching and no thought of giving in; and by what seemed almost a miracle to those outside these Islands, though we ourselves never doubted it, we now find ourselves in a position where I say that we can be sure that we have only to persevere to conquer.[7]

To persevere, to endure; so how in the world does that happen? First, we need to count the cost. Jesus said this very clearly:

> *And whoever does not bear his cross and come after Me cannot be My disciple. For which of you, intending to build a tower, does not sit down first and count the cost, whether he has enough to finish it...*[8]

Calculate what is going to take; and I want to tell you friends, it's going to take everything. If you were expecting a seeker-friendly feel-good message, you won't find it because this will cost you everything. I do not come and say flippantly that if you receive Jesus Christ as your Lord and Savior then everything is going to be wonderful from then on; though it certainly is wonderful. Yes, it is, and is there really any other choice? No; there is no other choice, but we need to be honest, and we need to sit down and say, "Am I willing to do this?" Or, will your decision be that the price is too high?

> *After this many of his disciples turned back and no longer walked with him. So Jesus said to the twelve, "Do you want to go away as well?"[9]*

We need to be active:

> *Submit yourselves therefore to God. Resist the devil, and he will flee from you.[10]*

> *Therefore take up the whole armor of God, that you may be able to withstand in the evil day, and having done all, to stand firm.[11]*

We have to stand; to stand; to stand against and resist, whether in deed or work; we plant our feet and will not be moved. I am convinced that He is the God in the universe, that Jesus is His Son by the power of the Holy Spirit. I am convinced, I stand and I will never be moved. We need to resist; we need to be cleaned up for the power to flow.

Many years ago I'd already been doing deliverances for a long time, and a man that I met in North Pole, Alaska (not the North Pole, but the city) called and said, "I have a verse for you, but do you know what it means?

> *That evening they brought to him many who were oppressed by demons, and he cast out the spirits with a word and healed all who were sick.*[12]

Isn't that amazing? How did He do it? He did it with a word, and I knew the Lord was saying to me that I needed to start doing deliverances by saying a word; and I'd say the word and I could feel the evil coming off the person, sometimes for up to three days, and it was exhausting. I found something out just a couple weeks ago because I was pondering what had been happening to me when I saw this verse with something hidden that I'd never seen before in my life:

> *Already you are clean because of the word that I have spoken to you.*[13]

I realized that Jesus did a total deliverance on the disciples because He is Jesus, the Anointed One. That's what Christ means, the Anointed One, and when He said that word the disciples were totally clean and the power of God could now flow through them. No one told me about that part.

All we did as pastors was preach to people to have more faith; and do this, do this, do this. We didn't understand, you see, it's not about what we do; it's about what He does in setting us free so that we can be vessels of his power. We need to work at getting cleaned up because the resistance is from the enemy, and we need to be cleaned up both personally and generationally. We are not going to operate in His power until we're cleaned up; but I did not understand this even after many years of doing this. But then something happened to me on May 30, 2020. Covid had already begun when the Lord told us that we were to have a meeting on Pentecost. It was a Saturday evening, and I realized that I could go to jail because we were going to have a church meeting during Covid. If you recall, that was the year when everyone was saying that the Holy Spirit was going to come and there would be signs and wonders and miracles; it would be wonderful. We came together, and everybody arrived with great expectations sounds and lights and power. We were sitting there waiting, and a friend of mine got up and came over and asked to stand in front of me. I said yes, so she did; and making a prophetic motion with her hands she said, "The Lord says, 'I am going to clean out your DNA.'" I was thrown back into my chair under the power God and realized I was going through a deliverance. Now, keep in mind, we've already had all these books and prayer manuals published, and had clearly already experienced a lot of cleaning up. I first thought it was going to go on for a week, then for two weeks; well maybe it would last twenty-one days. But it was still going, and I can't tell you how exhausting it was. Every morning I would wake up, and it was continuing. Beyond tired of the deliverance, I was trying meanwhile to be a good husband, father and grandfather; and trying to live a normal life. But, time passed, and twenty-one days extended past forty days; and the first round lasted four hundred days before there was a brief respite. Then it continued some more, until it reached eight-hundred-thirty-nine days of deliverance. It was one thing after another as the Lord would show us something new, and there would be more deliverance. I held to the thought:

> *For I am sure that neither death nor life, nor angels nor rulers, nor things present nor things to come, nor powers, nor height nor depth, nor anything else in all*

> *creation, will be able to separate us from the love of God in Christ Jesus our Lord.*[14]

It continued again, throughout all of last year (2022), but finally ended on my birthday this year, January 12th, after nine-hundred-fifty-seven days. I grew up in a Christian home and accepted the Lord when I was six years old. I do not say this to brag, for there was nothing to brag about here. Rather, this is to inform you that you need to take responsibility to get cleaned up, because if you want the power to come you need to be cleaned up. I had no idea that I was in such a mess!

Everything changed for me on March 26, 2023, during a powerful service at Mountain View Community Church in Hawaii in which the Holy Spirit was formally invited and welcomed into the church. I began feeling the Father, the Son and the Holy Spirit continually, but I don't think that happens just for me, but is a goal for all of us. We need to spread the word to all Christians, "Do you know you need to be cleaned up so the power can flow." It has to happen; and dying to self is necessary.

I was given a book before everything fell apart in the church where this all began, and the book is *A Tale of Three Kings* by a man named Gene Edwards. It's the kind of book that you want to throw across the hall into a wall, stomp on it, and tear it apart. The story is about Saul, David and Solomon, but the central character is David and how he left the throne when he was attacked by his son, Absalom. Essentially, David was dying to his position, his kingdom:

> *Then the king said to Zadok, "Carry the ark of God back into the city. If I find favor in the eyes of the LORD, he will bring me back and let me see both it and his dwelling*

place. But if he says, 'I have no pleasure in you,' behold, here I am, let him do to me what seems good to him." [15]

David's example is what it looks like to stand. To stand is to be obedient to Him, to refuse to budge. The whole armor of God is put on so you can stand, looking forward:

I press on toward the goal for the prize of the upward call of God in Christ Jesus. Let those of us who are mature think this way, and if in anything you think otherwise, God will reveal that also to you. [16]

We press forward, we look forward, we see the goal. The door for me is I go to heaven and He says, "Well done, My good and faithful son." That's my goal.

We need to decide. Think about going to the beach on a hot August day, looking at the cool, inviting water, and it's very, very tempting. So we go and put our toe into the ocean, and we're convinced that this is a refreshing idea and yes, it'd be really good to cool off. But there's a step beyond being convinced – it's being committed enough to jump in.

Have you dived in? Have you counted the cost of discipleship?

About a hundred-fifty years ago there was a great revival in Wales. As a result of this, many missionaries went to northeast India, including some American Baptists. As they witnessed to a tribe of head hunters, a man and his family became convinced and husband, wife and two children gave their lives to Jesus. The village chief was very, very angry, and brought them before the tribe and commanded them to renounce Jesus or face execution. The man replied, "I have decided to follow Jesus." Enraged, the chief ordered the archers to kill his two children and they were killed. As both boys lay dead, the chief asked, "Will you now renounce Jesus?" The response, "Though no one joins me, still I will follow," and his wife was shot dead. The chief was irate and demanded, "If you do not renounce Jesus, I will now kill you." And the final response, "The cross before me the world behind me, no turning back," and he was killed; but then something amazing happened. The chief said, "If this man is willing to do this for a man who lived two thousand years ago, then I will follow this Jesus;" and so he accepted Christ and the whole village became Christians.

You see, Apostle Paul said, "I'm an example to you, and I, Paul Cox, say that I'm also an example to you. Will you finally decide to really follow Jesus, no turning back no turning back?

Considering this message, I thought that it really ends on a heavy note, but I then had the thought about sales commercials on television. Don't you just love them? They say, "But wait if you act now you too can…" And this is the good news here; if you act now, you can have joy, you can have purpose, you could have an abundant life, you have meaning; you can have hope for your marriage, hope for your family, hope for the church; you can have all this if you'll just decide to really follow Jesus.

---

[1] 1 Corinthians 15:58

[2] 2 Corinthians 6:4-5

[3] Hebrews 10:32-36

[4] Hebrews 12:1-2

[5] 1 Peter 2:21

[6] 1 Corinthians 12:12-13 NKJV

[7] https://www.school-for-champions.com/speeches/churchill_never_give_in.htm#Text

[8] Luke 14:27-28
[9] John 6:66
[10] James 4:7
[11] Ephesians 6:13
[12] Matthew 8:16
[13] John 15:3
[14] Romans 8:38-39
[15] 1 Samuel 15:25-26
[16] Philippians 3:14-15

Chapter Two:
WHAT? I HAVE TO DIE???

In a video game, the levels are progressive, with each one requiring more and more skill; and the avatar of the player must die repeatedly to move from one level to the next and eventually, hopefully, win the game. In Bible days, there were no video games, but apparently Paul understood the concept anyway:

> *Not that I have already obtained this or am already perfect, but I press on to make it my own, because Christ Jesus has made me his own. Brothers, I do not consider that I have made it my own. But one thing I do: forgetting what lies behind and straining forward to what lies ahead, I press on toward the goal for the prize of the upward call of God in Christ Jesus. Let those of us who are mature think this way, and if in anything you think otherwise, God will reveal that also to you. Only let us hold true to what we have attained.*[1]

> *Therefore, since we are surrounded by so great a cloud of witnesses, let us also lay aside every weight, and sin which clings so closely, and let us run with endurance the race that is set before us, looking to Jesus, the founder and perfecter of our faith, who for the joy that was set before him endured the cross, despising the shame, and is seated at the right hand of the throne of God.*[2]

The Christian 'game' or 'race' is a progressive adventure of the practicing that which we've learned, which in the context of this book is perseverance, enduring faith, moving into His rest, knowing God, and moving deeper and deeper into His stillness. But wait, there's more! However, unlike the monetary cost to get in on the highly taunted products of an infomercial, the price of God's amazing blessings is a lot more difficult. Oh yes, the benefits far outweigh the cost; but many refuse to pay it because with the fullness of His promises come an ever-increasing call to put aside, to die, to all that we hold dear. We must die to self, as the Bible both instructs and illustrates; and Jesus' own words should be our first clue:

> *And he said to all, "If anyone would come after me, let him deny himself and take up his cross daily and follow me. For whoever would save his life will lose it, but whoever loses his life for my sake will save it. For what does it profit a man if he gains the whole world and loses or forfeits himself?*[3]

Hmmm, think about it a minute. What does a cross imply? Death, painful death; and if we really want to follow Him, we have to die. The 'nuts and bolts' of that were expounded on by New Testament writers:

> *For through the law I died to the law, so that I might live to God. I have been crucified with Christ. It is no longer I who live, but Christ who lives in me. And the life I now live in the flesh I live by faith in the Son of God, who loved me and gave himself for me.*[4]

> *We know that our old self was crucified with him in order that the body of sin might be brought to nothing, so that we would no longer be enslaved to sin. For one who has died has been set free from sin. Now if we have died with Christ, we believe that we will also live with him.*[5]

> *And those who belong to Christ Jesus have crucified the flesh with its passions and desires.*[6]

Yep. We have to die; we must be crucified with Christ so that He can live victoriously within us:

> *But far be it from me to boast except in the cross of our Lord Jesus Christ, by which the world has been crucified to me, and I to the world.*[7]

It's crystal clear that we have to die, to be crucified with Him, but how does that happen?

> *Put to death therefore what is earthly in you: sexual immorality, impurity, passion, evil desire, and covetousness, which is idolatry. On account of these the wrath of God is coming. In these you too once walked, when you were living in them. But now you must put them all away: anger, wrath, malice, slander, and obscene talk from your mouth.*[8]

What does that mean? What does that look like? There are many biblical examples, but to keep it simple let's look at just two. From the Old Testament, Abraham died to his son, Isaac; the young man upon whom rested all of God's promises to make him a great nation. We all know the story; we know what happened, God stepped in and spared Isaac's life. In dying to self, to his own heart's desires, Abraham both passed a test of faith and became an inspiration to every child of God from that point forward.

From the New Testament, consider Stephen. He counted his life as nothing, and joyfully proclaimed Jesus to the crowds who would momentarily stone him to death. But think about who was standing there, not only watching but holding the coats of the rock-throwers. It was Saul, the biggest persecutor of the Church who eventually became the best-known evangelist in history, the Apostle Paul. Could it be that with Steven's death a seed was planted in

Paul; a seed that germinated on the road to Damascus when he encountered Jesus? Probably, because it's very clear that Paul never forgot from whence he came:

> *I persecuted this Way to the death, binding and delivering to prison both men and women, as the high priest and the whole council of elders can bear me witness. From them I received letters to the brothers, and I journeyed toward Damascus to take those also who were there and bring them in bonds to Jerusalem to be punished.*[9]

So far so good, but let's get real. What does dying-to-self look like today? How can we relate to stories that are ancient history?

In my own life, the Lord has required me to die over and over to the things I hold most dear. It started years ago when He wouldn't relent until I gave Him my son, which was the hardest thing He's ever asked me to give up, but in retrospect also the most rewarding. I've had to relinquish control (die) to my marriage, my health and that of my family, finances, relationships, homes, jobs, and pretty much every desire and perceived need. All self-driven plans have had to go out the window, as happened again today. Let me be clear, dying to the world is not a one-shot deal.

Currently, my husband and I are facing several very difficult challenges, which just two days ago we handed over to the Lord. But last night, and again this morning, as my mind was going round and round looking for possible solutions, I began speaking to my husband about possibilities. Within minutes, I felt myself becoming more and more distressed and said, "Enough. I need to go and pray before I can talk about it any longer." We were both tired so we'd laid down to rest awhile, and at some point I had the sense of the Lord whispering, "Get up and have some coffee, and I will speak to you." I must admit, I questioned if that was Him or not, but what did I have to lose? A few minutes later, having coffee with the Lord at my desk, I wrote down some insights into our situation that resonated, and then thought I heard, "Break free." Of course, I questioned that too but He wasn't finished:

> (God) Break free of all that ties you down. You were made to soar like the eagles, so break free.

> (Barb) How? I assume this happens in the Spirit, but how? I don't know what is holding me down.

> (God) Be still and know that I am God. Wait. Practice what you preach.

Ouch! Immediately, I let go of my 'stuff' and found myself engulfed in His stillness. There in that place of knowing, I began to read the scriptures I had planned for today, and surprise, surprise (not!) God began speaking through them. I was studying 2 Corinthians 1 in the Tree of Life Version, which is a translation done by Messianic scholars. It is very close to my usual ESV, but with wording that was slightly different; just enough to catch my attention and really think about what I was reading. Following is the message which the Spirit spoke to my heart, which includes personalized-and-paraphrased portions of verses 2-4, 6, 9-10, 17, 19-21:

> Grace and peace from God our Father and Jesus the Messiah. I AM the Father of compassion and encouragement. I encourage you in every trouble, which produces patient endurance in your life. You live under a death sentence so that you might not rely on yourself but on God, who raises the dead. I

will continue to rescue you, for you have set your hope in Me.

Do you plan according to the flesh with every problem, debating between yes-versus-no, should-I versus shouldn't-I decisions? You shouldn't, because in Me it is always, "Yes," for in Me all My promises are "Yes." I am the God who establishes you in Jesus; who sets My seal upon you; who gives the Holy Spirit within your heart as My pledge."

Wow! There was no doubt now that it was God's voice I was hearing, and it is proven by a peace that rests deep within, assuring me that I don't have to work things out. It's just not my responsibility, because as long as I wait on Him, trust His word and be patient, He will always come through for me, and His words are not just for me; they are for every Believer. Our problem is that when God's promises aren't coming to pass as quickly as we think they should, we tend to want to help him along; and the enemy is adept at throwing doubts and temptations in our way. We begin to wonder what we did wrong, if we're hearing Him clearly, and all the when-and-why questions come pouring out of our hearts.

It all comes down to focus; are we looking at Him or at the things of the world? We are given a choice between living to those things we want, need, lack and expect; or dying to everything and living in peace, rest and stillness, knowing Him more intimately and experiencing His blessings.

Paul's thoughts:

One of my favorite sermons from Jesus is that of the prodigal son. The father gave the blessing (inheritance) out to both sons at the beginning.

Then the younger son asked for it, but when the father divided it up it meant that, technically, the father was dead because an inheritance is only given away when one dies. But the prodigal son came back and his father saw him and welcomed him home. With only two things left to give, a ring and a cloak, the father gave all he had to his son.

So now, the father, who represents the Heavenly Father, has just given away everything. What kind of crazy God is this? You look at the gods of history and they all require the sacrifices of the children; they require flagellation in which you must beat yourself. There are all sorts of misery in life; and yet this God of ours gives away everything. He's like some sort of mad used car salesman who comes and says, "Here come and take whatever you want. I've already paid for it; you can have it."

In the story, the prodigal son's father then killed a calf. I think this is one of the things that angered the older son because, since the inheritance had already been given away, Dad was probably killing his calf. It's like the older son was out in the mission field; laboring so hard, and so very tired and miserable; but he was working hard and was very religious, so he seemingly was doing everything right. But then he heard people laughing and having fun and wondered, "What is that going on when I am working so hard out here, and being so good and doing everything so perfectly?" So he sent his servant in to check it out. Then he also went and asked his dad to come out and explain things.

This parable is so absurd, and it had to be hilariously funny to the Jews. They were probably on the ground laughing, just because it is so stupid that any of this might have actually happened. You would never ask your father to come out and explain himself in that society.

But the father did come out and asked, "Now, what is your problem?" And the older son answered, "Well they are having fun in there while I have been slaving away, and you haven't given me anything."

What??? He got everything in the beginning of the parable, right? He already had it all; and not only that, but he had a larger inheritance than his younger brother because the older one always got the most.

It's as if his father turned to him and said, "Son, you know everybody has died in this parable. I died at the beginning of the story; now your brother has died and the calf is dead. Why don't you drop dead and join the party?"

The Kingdom of God is like a party made up of dead people; all of them just having a great time enjoying the Kingdom, and a crazy Father who is so loving that He gives everything away, even His only begotten Son.

The final challenge then, is:

I appeal to you therefore, brothers, by the mercies of God, to present your bodies as a living sacrifice, holy and acceptable to God, which is your spiritual worship. Do not be conformed to this world, but be transformed by the renewal of your mind, that by testing you may discern what is the will of God, what is good and acceptable and perfect.[10]

This then, is the choice for every one of us; a choice that must often be made on a daily basis; a choice to remain attached to the things of the world or to die and join the party.

---

[1] Philippians 3:12-16

[2] Hebrews 12:1-2

[3] Luke 9:23-25

[4] Galatians 2:19-20

[5] Romans 6:6-8

[6] Galatians 5:24

[7] Galatians 6:14

[8] Colossians 3:5-8

[9] Acts 22:4-5

[10] Romans 12:1-2

CHAPTER THREE:
COUNTING THE COST

If you're anything like me, you've analyzed the pros and cons many times of purchasing something expensive. In the end we've experienced one of two results; either the item was well worth the price we paid, or an unwise decision brought disappointment and regret, sometimes for years. No doubt, most of us could tell many stories about our expensive mistakes!

Jesus spoke of the wisdom of counting the cost of discipleship:

> *If anyone comes to me and does not hate his own father and mother and wife and children and brothers and sisters, yes, and even his own life, he cannot be my disciple. Whoever does not bear his own cross and come after me cannot be my disciple. For which of you, desiring to build a tower, does not first sit down and count the cost, whether he has enough to complete it? Otherwise, when he has laid a foundation and is not able to finish, all who see it begin to mock him, saying, 'This man began to build and was not able to finish.' Or what king, going out to encounter another king in war, will not sit down first and deliberate whether he is able with ten thousand to meet him who comes against him with twenty thousand? And if not, while the other is yet a great way off, he sends a delegation and asks for terms of peace. So therefore, any one of you who does not renounce all that he has cannot be my disciple.*[1]

Like the twelve who Jesus called, everyone today must respond to His summons, the first of which is to believe and receive Him as our savior. Those who say no will count the cost of their denial of Jesus throughout eternity. Among those who have accepted Him, the next step is to respond each time the Lord calls; kind of like God did with Samuel, who didn't understand why he was hearing his name until Eli explained it to him:

> *Then the LORD called Samuel, and he said, "Here I am!" and ran to Eli and said, "Here I am, for you called me." But he said, "I did not call; lie down again." So he went and lay down. And the LORD called again, "Samuel!" and Samuel arose and went to Eli and said, "Here I am, for you called me." But he said, "I did not call, my son; lie down again." Now Samuel did not yet know the LORD, and the word of the LORD had not yet been revealed to him. And the LORD called Samuel again the third time. And he arose and went to Eli and said, "Here I am, for you called me." Then Eli perceived that the LORD was calling the boy. Therefore Eli said to Samuel, "Go, lie down, and if he calls you, you shall say, 'Speak, LORD, for your servant hears.' " So Samuel went and lay down in his place. And the LORD came and stood, calling as at other times, "Samuel! Samuel!" And Samuel said, "Speak, for your servant hears." Then the LORD said to Samuel, "Behold, I am about to do a thing in Israel at which the two ears of everyone who hears it will tingle.*[2]

Just as Samuel had to learn to discern God's voice, so do we; and it often requires a lot of practice. Is it worth it? I have to say yes, because nothing is more precious to me than hearing the voice of my Lord and living in communion with Him.

Moving on in the Christian journey, there are likely many calls; perhaps regarding any major life decision, a call to a particular ministry or job, a call to move across the country. Abraham could certainly relate to that one!

> *Now the LORD said to Abram, "Go from your country and your kindred and your father's house to the land that I will show you. And I will make of you a great nation, and I will bless you and make your name great, so that you will be a blessing. I will bless those who bless you, and him who dishonors you I will curse, and in you all the families of the earth shall be blessed." So Abram went, as the LORD had told him, and Lot went with him. Abram was seventy-five years old when he departed from Haran.[3]*

Few of us are called at the ripe old age of 75, but then none of us live to be 175 either. We may be more like Jeremiah:

> *Now the word of the LORD came to me, saying, "Before I formed you in the womb I knew you, and before you were born I consecrated you; I appointed you a prophet to the nations." Then I said, "Ah, Lord GOD! Behold, I do not know how to speak, for I am only a youth." But the LORD said to me, "Do not say, 'I am only a youth'; for to all to whom I send you, you shall go, and whatever I command you, you shall speak. Do not be afraid of them, for I am with you to deliver you, declares the LORD."* [4]

That was more like my experience, for I remember very clearly responding to God's clarion call for me to enter into fulltime Christian service when I was just 12 years old. I was committed, and I also clearly recall singing such hymns as *So Send I You* with a passion. I thought I had a plan to serve Him, but mine was not fully aligned with His, and that set me up for a lot of disappointment. As the Children of Israel wandered in the desert, so did I wander, literally, for 40 years before I began to have an inkling of what that call on my life might mean.

Then there's Isaiah:

> *And I heard the voice of the Lord saying, "Whom shall I send, and who will go for us?" Then I said, "Here I am! Send me."* [5]

With both Jeremiah and Isaiah, God made it beyond clear right up front that the task He was asking them to do would not be easy, that the people to whom they were sent would not listen, yet they both agreed to obey Him.

But isn't the Christian life supposed to be easy? Don't many churches teach that once we are saved all of our problems will be resolved? Sadly, may churches do teach that since all was taken care of at the cross, once we accept Jesus, our lives will be fine going forward and all we need to do is endure until we all get to Heaven. When I think of that, I wonder if God had a chuckle or two over the popular song from 1967, *I Never Promised You a Rose Garden*, which reflects unexpected difficulties, and rain along with the sunshine. After all, roses come with thorns, and those thorns are beneficial:

> As everyone knows, even the most beautiful rose has thorns. But why so? Believe it or not, a rose's thorns — technically called "prickles" — are extremely important for its survival. They do everything from helping rose bushes grow to keeping them safe from predators and casual flower-pickers.[6]

But, but, but... I've done my best to follow God's voice and to do only what I see the Father doing; and life has still blown up in my face! If that sentiment feels familiar, all I can say is that you've got company, Paul and me included. As always though, what does the Bible say? A quick look at Hebrews 11 again will illustrate the price the members of the Faith Hall of Fame had to pay, not to mention all of the original apostles and the multitudes of Christian martyrs in the early Church and continuing on down through the centuries to the present. But there's another biblical account in Judges 20 that recently brought it home to me again that there is a cost to discipleship, even when we are following the Lord and doing those things He assigned.

The tribe of Benjamin had been in rebellion against God, and the remainder of Israel came together in unity to go to war against their brother. They inquired of God and He told them what to do, yet in the ensuing battle Benjamin prevailed and 22,000 Israelites died. Their response:

> *And the people of Israel went up and wept before the* LORD *until the evening. And they inquired of the* LORD*, "Shall we again draw near to fight against our brothers, the people of Benjamin?" And the* LORD *said, "Go up against them."* [7]

OK, maybe things would be better this time, right? Wrong! They obeyed and this time 18,000 died. This is probably where most of us would really, really begin to doubt God, probably blaming Him and making a decision to just walk away because that would surely be easier than facing the possibility of death. To their credit, the Israelites didn't simply abandon ship:

> *Then all the people of Israel, the whole army, went up and came to Bethel and wept. They sat there before the* LORD *and fasted that day until evening, and offered burnt offerings and peace offerings before the* LORD*. And the people of Israel inquired of the* LORD *(for the ark of the*

> *covenant of God was there in those days, and Phinehas the son of Eleazar, son of Aaron, ministered before it in those days), saying, "Shall we go out once more to battle against our brothers, the people of Benjamin, or shall we cease?" And the* LORD *said, "Go up, for tomorrow I will give them into your hand."* [8]

And so it was, God did deliver an astounding victory; and if we remain faithful to our calling, He will always remain faithful to us:

> *Now may the God of peace himself sanctify you completely, and may your whole spirit and soul and body be kept blameless at the coming of our Lord Jesus Christ. He who calls you is faithful; he will surely do it.*[9]

> *Do not fear what you are about to suffer. Behold, the devil is about to throw some of you into prison, that you may be tested, and for ten days you will have tribulation. Be faithful unto death, and I will give you the crown of life.*[10]

There's a children's song, *Dare to be a Daniel*, the chorus of which challenges us with the words:

> Dare to be a Daniel!
> Dare to stand alone!
> Dare to have a purpose firm!
> Dare to make it known!

I'd go a step further and say that we should dare to be not only a Daniel but an Abraham, a Moses, a Jeremiah, an Isaac, an Esther, a Ruth, or any one of numerous other Bible heroes who chose to say yes to God and to endure and overcome regardless of the cost.

Whom among us will declare, "Here I am; send me, Lord"? It may not be easy, but it will be worth it!

---

[1] Luke 14:26-33
[2] 1 Samuel 3:4-11
[3] Genesis 12:1-4
[4] Jeremiah 1:4-8
[5] Isaiah 6:8
[6] https://www.wikihow.com/Why-Does-a-Rose-Have-Thorns
[7] Judges 20:23
[8] Judges 20:26-28
[9] 1 Thessalonians 5:23-24
[10] Revelation 2:10

Chapter Four
God's Waiting Room

Whom among us cannot relate to the all-too-familiar idiom, 'hurry up and wait'? Few, if any, I imagine. It's a phrase that may have originated sometime in the 1940s by members of the military who received orders to complete a task, only to then have to wait, wait and wait some more before it was acted on. But military aside, the concept is familiar to all of us who have rushed to get to an appointment on time, only to sit and twiddle our thumbs waiting for others who were running behind. We've all probably waited for everything from medications to resolve physical infirmities to promises that haven't been fulfilled; the list is practically endless.

In the fast-paced society in which we live we've been more conditioned to encounter the antonyms of waiting; and we're in a hurry, on a fast track, in the fast lane or chomping at the bit. Such a pattern in our lives can, and often does, conflict with God's instructions:

> *Be still before the* Lord *and wait patiently for him; fret not yourself over the one who prospers in his way, over the man who carries out evil devices!* [1]

When the Lord says to wait and we forge ahead of Him, we're destined for disappointment. King Saul learned that the hard way:

> *Then go down before me to Gilgal. And behold, I am coming down to you to offer burnt offerings and to sacrifice peace offerings. Seven days you shall wait, until I come to you and show you what you shall do." ... He waited seven days, the time appointed by Samuel. But*

> *Samuel did not come to Gilgal, and the people were scattering from him. So Saul said, "Bring the burnt offering here to me, and the peace offerings." And he offered the burnt offering. As soon as he had finished offering the burnt offering, behold, Samuel came. And Saul went out to meet him and greet him. Samuel said, "What have you done?" And Saul said, "When I saw that the people were scattering from me, and that you did not come within the days appointed, and that the Philistines had mustered at Michmash, I said, 'Now the Philistines will come down against me at Gilgal, and I have not sought the favor of the LORD.' So I forced myself, and offered the burnt offering." And Samuel said to Saul, "You have done foolishly. You have not kept the command of the LORD your God, with which he commanded you. For then the LORD would have established your kingdom over Israel forever. But now your kingdom shall not continue. The LORD has sought out a man after his own heart, and the LORD has commanded him to be prince over his people, because you have not kept what the LORD commanded you."*[2]

King David was that man after God's own heart, but after Samuel anointed him as God's new choice for king he had to wait for years while the jealous Saul desperately sought to kill him. David learned to wait, and his was a voice of experience:

> *Indeed, none who wait for you shall be put to shame; they shall be ashamed who are wantonly treacherous. Make me to know your ways, O LORD; teach me your paths. Lead me in your truth and teach me, for you are the God of my salvation; for you I wait all the day long... Consider how many are my foes, and with what violent hatred they hate me. Oh, guard my soul, and deliver me! Let me not be put to shame, for I take refuge in you. May*

integrity and uprightness preserve me, for I wait for you.[3]

Wait for the LORD; be strong, and let your heart take courage; wait for the LORD![4]

Save me, O God! For the waters have come up to my neck. I sink in deep mire, where there is no foothold; I have come into deep waters, and the flood sweeps over me. I am weary with my crying out; my throat is parched. My eyes grow dim with waiting for my God.[5]

When the Lord impressed me to write a chapter about waiting, I delved into my old notes and was surprised to see that He first began the prompting in August 2020:

> Waiting was on my mind yesterday as I considered staying up from 12-3 AM to wait each night, but that didn't happen and I don't have any clear inclination I should; but I wonder if I am to write about waiting. As I pondered, I had a sense of being in a waiting room, which seemed as of the world is the waiting room of eternity in which God eliminates ancient evil.

The notes in that journal entry continued with a lot of other thoughts about waiting, many of which have finally found a home in this chapter. But what surprised me even more was the fact that I've had at least four dreams about God's waiting rooms over the years.

About fifteen years so, my dream took me to a waiting room in a doctor's office (the Great Physician!) where I watched as lots of other people came in. They were of various nationalities and languages; seemingly people with whom I would have little in common. But then the singing started as a small group of young men who looked like they could have cone straight out of a gang began to croon in perfect harmony. Gradually, one after another everyone who was waiting also began singing; their voices also harmonious and producing in unity one of the most beautiful sounds one could imagine. I believe this represents God's Church coming together in one accord to worship as we wait together for Jesus' return.

Then, ten years ago there was dream in which I was in some sort of vehicle with an open convertible top; and there was a second person with me whose identity was unclear. At the time, I had been asking the Lord for the ability to see more clearly in the Spirit; so as this vehicle sped faster and faster across the landscape – literally flying a few feet off the ground - I was thrilled that I could see much that was happening in a beautiful forest, sights that I knew wouldn't be apparent to many people. I kept exclaiming to the other person, "Did you see that?" over and over. Suddenly, the vehicle took off like a rocket as we were launched high into the atmosphere. I looked down, and below us were lots of dinosaurs – big ones, with their giant heads reaching up as high as they could and their terrible jaws snapping as they tried to reach us. But they couldn't! I was laughing joyfully because it was abundantly clear that we had been taken out of their reach and they couldn't touch us. Meanwhile, we were still moving even higher. Finally, we apparently reached our destination because suddenly we were no longer flying but found ourselves inside a circular waiting room where there were two beds, which symbolize the rest of the Lord. We began by looking around at pictures on the walls and exploring this new place, and then laid down to relax on the beds. Another 'suddenly' occurred as a door opened and the brightest light I've ever seen engulfed us. The Light of the World had come.

During a time of prayer about four years ago, I had a sense of being in a very large, circular waiting room, and wondered if it was a court. At first, it was as if I was the only one there, but then two or three seemed to be present. Wondering if I was imagining things, I had a conversation with the Lord:

> Barb: Lord, please remove any sense of self from my understanding and totally remove my thoughts if they are not of You. What is this place? OK, so this is my sense of Your response and please, again, erase any thought that is not of You.
>
> God: Yes, this is one of My courts, a place where my servants do come to wait. You cannot see what happens in the inner rooms, which remain closed until the fulness of My time comes. You often counsel others to wait, and you have often had to wait; but rest assured, I do hear the cries of Your heart and still you must wait. You have been right about your personal crucible, but I will redeem it, I will redeem it! Wait; be still and wait, and trust Me. Would that this and many other such rooms were full of My people who are willing to wait. Pray for that to happen. You cannot even begin to comprehend the power of waiting or what changes would occur if My rooms were packed with waiters.
>
> Barb: I suddenly had a sense of 'a kind of hush' and prayed: Lord, please cause a righteous hush to fall upon God's people; like a parent soothing a child with comforting words, and the child calming down in their arms and waiting because they know they can trust the parent. May it be so all over the

world, Lord; may Your people who are called by your name hear Your voice calling us into Your presence and Your waiting rooms.

Sometimes we find ourselves sitting in God's waiting room, wondering if He's forgotten about us. Perhaps He's given us an instruction that needed to be done right away and we did what was asked; but now we're stuck waiting – again - with no visible evidence either of why we needed to do what He assigned or what comes next. What then? How do we respond when God asks us to continue to wait? Perhaps we should heed David's wise advice:

Wait for the LORD and keep his way, and he will exalt you to inherit the land; you will look on when the wicked are cut off.[6]

But is it worth the wait? Scriptures confirm that it is:

I waited patiently for the LORD; he inclined to me and heard my cry.[7]

Blessed is the one who listens to me, watching daily at my gates, waiting beside my doors.[8]

It will be said on that day, "Behold, this is our God; we have waited for him, that he might save us. This is the LORD; we have waited for him; let us be glad and rejoice in his salvation." [9]

Even youths shall faint and be weary, and young men shall fall exhausted; but they who wait for the LORD shall renew their strength; they shall mount up with wings like eagles; they shall run and not be weary; they shall walk and not faint.[10]

> *The LORD is good to those who wait for him, to the soul who seeks him. It is good that one should wait quietly for the salvation of the LORD.*[11]

A few weeks ago, I had another conversation with the Lord:

> Barb: My mind knows You're here; my heart knows you're here. I need to feel Your presence. I will wait for You.
>
> God: How long will you wait?
>
> Barb: I want to say as long as it takes, for this moment as well as other times when I sense a need to go still and be silent. I assume You will prolong the time today with no interruptions until we're finished; but, are you speaking of longer waits?
>
> God: Yes, I am. Keep thinking.
>
> Barb: I'll wait for Your return, Your direction, fulfilled prophecies, answered prayers and new downloads and revelation. I want to say I'll wait for healing to begin in my family as has been prophesied, but if I'm honest, I wonder if am I doubting that those healings will actually happen.
>
> God: You wondered earlier if this conversation is about your individual faith. Yes, it is. You do not doubt My ability to heal; you only wonder if/when I will heal. So, instead of accepting the lie of the enemy that you are doubting Me and allowing the plague of self-doubt to assault you, step into enduring faith. You just almost prayed for Me to increase your faith, but caught yourself because you understand the principle of the mustard seed. You have all the faith you need, so use it to wait.

Barb: Ahh, I need to embrace the wait; so these willing-to-wait issues are being addressed. Yes, Lord, and I'm willing to wait for my whole 'laundry list' of promises that are still on the shelf.

God: Be faithful in the small things; I will bless them; and in the fulness of My time you will step into the more. Wait. Remember, *One who is faithful in a very little is also faithful in much.*[12]

Our battle cry should be:

I wait for the LORD, my soul waits, and in his word I hope; my soul waits for the Lord more than watchmen for the morning, more than watchmen for the morning.[13]

It appears that waiting and faith are inexplicable tied together in ways that cannot be fully explained or understood, so stay tuned.

---

[1] Psalm 37:7

[2] 1 Samuel 10:8, 13:8-14

[3] Psalm 25:3-5, 19-21

[4] Psalm 27:14

[5] Psalm 69:1-3

[6] Psalm 37:34

[7] Psalm 40:1

[8] Proverbs 8:34

[9] Isaiah 25:9

[10] Isaiah 40:30-31

[11] Lamentations 3:25-26

[12] Luke 16:10a

[13] Psalm 130:5-6

CHAPTER FIVE:
CARS & FAITH

Recently, we experienced a dire transportation crisis in which both of our vehicles were disabled. Our everyday, dependable 2011 Expedition was flashing warning lights at us, and it was finally determined that the brake module had failed. Turned out, we were number 900 on the wait list for a part that hadn't even been manufactured yet. Then there was our back-up, a 2008 Toyota in need of so many expensive repairs that we only drove it for short, local errands. In general, while everything we need is within a one-to-five-mile radius from home, there was no way it would have been safe to drive either vehicle on the freeway. But – a big BUT - we had a couple of important places we were scheduled to go, each of which would require about a 200-mile round trip. What to do?

Perhaps the least expensive option would be to have the Toyota repaired, so my husband consulted with our auto repair shop, only to discover that there were even more issues than we thought. It just wasn't worth the money required to fix such an old vehicle, no matter that the body looked almost new and the interior was still in very good shape.

Again, what to do? Prayer had been ongoing, but thus far with no clear answers. Isn't that the way life's challenges often seem? Difficult problems without obvious solutions routinely persist in spite of prayer; and that's where faith comes in. Whether the issue is a relatively minor need like ours for reliable transportation, more serious issues such as relationships, schools, jobs, etc.; or the desperate needs brought about through loss or infirmity; the solutions always rest in waiting on the Lord and holding onto faith in Him.

Ultimately for us, the Lord provided someone who wanted to buy the Toyota for more than we ever thought we could get, and then intervened to provide a new-to-us used car that looks and runs like new. It is a gift from Him, one that we couldn't have dreamed of; and it came about through prayer and faith that He would supply our need. But the point of our story isn't so much to talk about what happened with our transportation problem, but to introduce an analogy between cars and faith using our new car as an example. They have much in common.

We see our car as a gift from God; as is faith:

> *For by grace you have been saved through faith. And this is not your own doing; it is the gift of God.* [1]

It's very comforting to know that we have reliable transportation, secure in the knowledge that we can safely drive to our destinations. Faith is the very basis of security with God, and through faith we can proclaim with the psalmists:

> *I have set the LORD always before me; because he is at my right hand, I shall not be shaken.* [2]

> *You who have made me see many troubles and calamities will revive me again; from the depths of the earth you will bring me up again. You will increase my greatness and comfort me again.* [3]

Our car allows us to travel, to seek out new destinations and enjoy the ride. By faith, we also travel into the unseen realms of the Lord:

> *But God, being rich in mercy, because of the great love with which he loved us, even when we were dead in our trespasses, made us alive together with Christ – by grace you have been saved – and raised us up with him and seated us with him in the heavenly places in Christ Jesus, so that in the coming ages he might show the immeasurable riches of his grace in kindness toward us in Christ Jesus.[4]*

> *If then you have been raised with Christ, seek the things that are above, where Christ is, seated at the right hand of God. Set your minds on things that are above, not on things that are on earth. For you have died, and your life is hidden with Christ in God. When Christ who is your life appears, then you also will appear with him in glory.[5]*

Our car comes with unexpected upgrades that we've not had in other cars. Faith enables us to experience upgrades in our lives, which we could have never anticipated before we knew Jesus:

> *Though you have not seen him, you love him. Though you do not now see him, you believe in him and rejoice with joy that is inexpressible and filled with glory, obtaining the outcome of your faith, the salvation of your souls.[6]*

> *For everyone who has been born of God overcomes the world. And this is the victory that has overcome the world – our faith.[7]*

A good car is both highly desired and a tremendous blessing. It's easy to forget that many people in the world are so poor they must still walk, ride a bicycle or depend on other people or animals to get from place to place. Faith is also highly desired, and it is a much greater blessing than any vehicle:

> *Now faith is the assurance of things hoped for, the conviction of things not seen. For by it the people of old received their commendation. By faith we understand that the universe was created by the word of God, so that what is seen was not made out of things that are visible.*[8]

When one has a reliable car, it can be used for good to help others. How much greater is the good that arises out of faith:

> *But the fruit produced by the Holy Spirit within you is divine love in all its varied expressions: joy that overflows, peace that subdues, patience that endures, kindness in action, a life full of virtue, faith that prevails, gentleness of heart, and strength of spirit. Never set the law above these qualities, for they are meant to be limitless.*[9]

Car ownership comes with tremendous responsibilities; one must understand and follow the rules of the road in order to remain safe. So it is with faith, a powerful weapon of righteousness when placed in God; but misplaced faith is very dangerous:

> *Claiming to be wise, they became fools, and exchanged the glory of the immortal God for images resembling mortal man and birds and animals and creeping things... And since they did not see fit to acknowledge God, God gave them up to a debased mind to do what ought not to be done. They were filled with all manner of unrighteousness, evil, covetousness, malice. They are full of envy, murder, strife, deceit, maliciousness. They are gossips, slanderers, haters of God, insolent, haughty, boastful, inventors of evil, disobedient to parents, foolish, faithless, heartless, ruthless*[10]

Both cars and faith may appear miraculous, perhaps impossible, to those who haven't experienced them.

Imagine the awestruck wonder of people who watched Model Ts chugging down the road. While some were awestruck, others wanted nothing to do with those new-fangled machines. Sadly, many people today doubt the reality of God and His promises; wanting nothing to do with Him, but the scriptures speak for themselves regarding the necessity of faith:

> *And without faith it is impossible to please him, for whoever would draw near to God must believe that he exists and that he rewards those who seek him.*[11]

Both cars and faith are useless without fuel. Clearly, there has to be a source of power for a car, which began with steam, transitioned to gasoline, and now has been expanded to include electricity. The source of faith, as well as other spiritual gifts, is the Holy Spirit:

> *For to one is given through the Spirit the utterance of wisdom, and to another the utterance of knowledge according to the same Spirit, to another faith by the same Spirit, to another gifts of healing by the one Spirit, to another the working of miracles, to another prophecy, to another the ability to distinguish between spirits, to another various kinds of tongues, to another the interpretation of tongues. All these are empowered by one and the same Spirit, who apportions to each one individually as he wills.*[12]

Faith is not something that just happens automatically; it comes packaged as small as a mustard seed, but Jesus said that mustard seed faith would move mountains. How is that even possible? By exercising our tiny faith, it grows through trial and error, again and again. But remember, with just a few words from the Lord, the heavens and the earth were created; imagine what just one of His words, encompassed in a mustard seed, can do when we respond by faith.

The results of my faith don't rest in me; for within myself there is no ability to move mountains. Rather, it's faith in the One who gave me the faith in the first place; it's faith in what He can do.

> *Not that I have already obtained this or am already perfect, but I press on to make it my own, because Christ Jesus has made me his own. Brothers, I do not consider that I have made it my own. But one thing I do: forgetting what lies behind and straining forward to what lies ahead, I press on toward the goal for the prize of the upward call of God in Christ Jesus.*[13]

---

[1] Ephesian 2:8

[2] Psalm 16:8

[3] Psalm 71:20-21

[4] Ephesians 2:5-7

[5] Colossians 3:1-4

[6] 1 Peter 1:8-9

[7] 1 John 5:4

[8] Hebrews 11:1-3

[9] Galatians 5:22-23 TPT

[10] Romans 1: 22-23, 28031

[11] Hebrews 11:6

[12] ! Corinthians 12:8-11

[13] Philippians 3:12-14

Chapter Six:
Defining Faith

Faith is a common theme throughout the Bible – from people like Enoch, Noah and Abraham in Genesis all the way to the Apostle John in Revelation. We talk about it a lot, but how should we define faith? The biblical definition is clear:

> *Now faith is the assurance of things hoped for, the conviction of things not seen.*[1]

There was a time not so long ago when the unseen realms were scoffed at; but that was before modern advances in science and technology, in tandem with popular entertainment that routinely explores unseen dimensions of time and space, changed the way people think. Nowadays, the conviction of things not seen isn't a wild idea at all; as long as it has nothing to do with the Bible that is, because then there is doubt galore.

Every Christian has practiced a leap of faith in receiving Jesus, a leap that boggles the minds of those who have either rejected Him or remain skeptical of God's promise of eternal life through His Son. Sadly too, many of these same Christians balk at the idea that **all** of God's promises and gifts remain relevant today, though the scriptures are clear:

> *God is not man, that he should lie, or a son of man, that he should change his mind. Has he said, and will he not do it? Or has he spoken, and will he not fulfill it?*[2]

> *Jesus Christ is the same yesterday and today and forever.*[3]

Do not be deceived, my beloved brothers. Every good gift and every perfect gift is from above, coming down from the Father of lights, with whom there is no variation or shadow due to change.[4]

One of the Lord's perfect gifts, the gift of faith, is listed among the Holy Spirit's nine gifts in 1 Corinthians 12:7-11,:

> 1 Corinthians 12:9 – faith - *pistis* (πίστις, 4102), "faith," has the secondary meaning of "an assurance or guarantee, e.g., Acts 17:31; by raising Christ from the dead, God has given "assurance" that the world will be judged by Him (the KJV margin, "offered faith" does not express the meaning). Cf. 1 Tim. 5:12, where "faith" means "pledge." See BELIEF, FAITH, FIDELITY.[5]

People who are blessed with the gift of faith have the ability to stand strong in the midst of life's storms. They might be described by a slightly modified use of the informal motto of the postal service, "With the help of God, neither snow nor rain nor heat nor gloom of night stays these Christians from the swift completion of their appointed rounds." If God said it, they believe it unquestioningly, and will not be dissuaded from His truths as recorded in the Bible. Their faith is both a source of hope for themselves during difficult times, and an encouragement to others. A favorite verse of many may be:

> *Therefore take up the whole armor of God, that you may be able to withstand in the evil day, and <u>having done all, to stand firm</u>.*[6]

I (Barbara) am fortunate to have heard the Lord's audible voice on one occasion, and in the instant after it happened I could already not explain what it sounded like other than to say the words were abundantly clear. I heard, "I have given you the gift of faith, for without it you would not have survived." Thus, my ministry is called *Standing in Faith*, and one of my books, *I'm Still Standing*. That isn't to say there is never a temptation to give up when things get tough; there is, but for me there is no other option but to hold onto His truth and stand firm. I share this here not to boast but to give God the glory for His gift; and to encourage others that if I could receive the gift of faith in my desperate state, so can any other believer. Each of us has been given a measure of faith, and each of us is capable of exercising that faith:

> *For by the grace given to me I say to everyone among you not to think of himself more highly than he ought to think, but to think with sober judgment, each according to the measure of faith that God has assigned.*[7]

Jesus routinely spoke of the need for faith and also mentioned time and again when He healed someone that it was their faith that made them well:

> *But if God so clothes the grass of the field, which today is alive and tomorrow is thrown into the oven, will he not much more clothe you, O you of little faith?*[8]

> *When he had entered Capernaum, a centurion came forward to him, appealing to him, "Lord, my servant is lying paralyzed at home, suffering terribly." And he said to him, "I will come and heal him." But the centurion replied, "Lord, I am not worthy to have you come under my roof, but only say the word, and my servant will be healed. For I too am a man under authority, with soldiers under me. And I say to one, 'Go,' and he goes, and to another, 'Come,' and he comes, and to my servant, 'Do this,' and he does it." When Jesus heard this, he marveled*

and said to those who followed him, "Truly, I tell you, with no one in Israel have I found such faith."[9]

And they went and woke him, saying, "Save us, Lord; we are perishing." And he said to them, "Why are you afraid, O you of little faith?" Then he rose and rebuked the winds and the sea, and there was a great calm.[10]

Then Jesus answered her, "O woman, great is your faith! Be it done for you as you desire." And her daughter was healed instantly.[11]

And Jesus answered, "O faithless and twisted generation, how long am I to be with you? How long am I to bear with you? Bring him here to me." And Jesus rebuked the demon, and it came out of him, and the boy was healed instantly. [12]

Perhaps the principle of use-it-or-lose-it might apply, which is what I think actually happened in my life:

Be watchful, stand firm in the faith, act like men, be strong.[13]

This was according to the eternal purpose that he has realized in Christ Jesus our Lord, in whom we have boldness and access with confidence through our faith in him.[14]

In all circumstances take up the shield of faith, with which you can extinguish all the flaming darts of the evil one.[15]

For, "Yet a little while, and the coming one will come and will not delay; but my righteous one shall live by faith, and if he shrinks back, my soul has no pleasure in him." But we are not of those who shrink back and are destroyed, but of those who have faith and preserve their souls.[16]

For everyone who has been born of God overcomes the world. And this is the victory that has overcome the world — our faith.[17]

Hebrews 11 not only defines faith but beautifully expounds on what it looked like in the lives of Old Testament saints. It's so inspiring, we include the whole chapter here:

Now faith is the assurance of things hoped for, the conviction of things not seen. For by it the people of old received their commendation. By faith we understand that the universe was created by the word of God, so that what is seen was not made out of things that are visible. By faith Abel offered to God a more acceptable sacrifice than Cain, through which he was commended as righteous, God commending him by accepting his gifts. And through his faith, though he died, he still speaks. By faith Enoch was taken up so that he should not see death, and he was not found, because God had taken him. Now before he was taken he was commended as having pleased God. And without faith it is impossible to please him, for whoever would draw near to God must believe that he exists and that he rewards those who seek him. By faith Noah, being warned by God concerning events as yet unseen, in reverent fear constructed an ark for the saving of his household. By this he condemned the world and became an heir of the righteousness that comes by faith. By faith Abraham obeyed when he was called to go out to a place that he was to receive as an inheritance. And he went out, not knowing where he was going. By faith he went to live in the land of promise, as in a foreign land, living in tents with Isaac and Jacob, heirs with him of the same promise. For he was looking forward to the city that has foundations, whose designer and builder is God. By faith Sarah herself received power to conceive, even when she was past the age, since she considered him faithful who had promised. Therefore from one man, and him as good as dead, were born descendants as many as the stars of heaven and as many as the innumerable grains of sand by the seashore. These all died in faith, not having received the things promised, but having seen them and greeted them from afar, and having acknowledged that they were strangers and exiles on the earth. For people who speak thus make it clear that they are seeking a homeland. If they had been thinking of that land from which they had gone out, they would have had opportunity to return. But as it is, they desire a better country, that is, a heavenly one. Therefore God is not ashamed to be called their God, for he has prepared for them a city. By faith Abraham, when he was tested, offered up Isaac, and he who had received the promises was in the act of offering up his only son, of whom it was said, "Through Isaac shall your offspring be named." He considered that God was able even to raise him from the dead, from which, figuratively speaking, he did receive him back. By faith Isaac invoked future blessings on Jacob and Esau. By faith Jacob, when dying, blessed each of the sons of Joseph, bowing in worship over the head of his staff. By faith Joseph, at the end of his life, made mention of the exodus of the Israelites and gave directions concerning his bones. By faith Moses, when he was born, was hidden for three months by his parents, because they saw that the child was beautiful, and they were not afraid of the king's edict. By faith Moses, when he was grown up, refused to be called the son of Pharaoh's daughter, choosing rather to be mistreated with the people of God than to enjoy the fleeting pleasures of sin. He considered the reproach of Christ greater wealth than the treasures of Egypt, for he was looking to the reward. By faith he left

Egypt, not being afraid of the anger of the king, for he endured as seeing him who is invisible. By faith he kept the Passover and sprinkled the blood, so that the Destroyer of the firstborn might not touch them. By faith the people crossed the Red Sea as on dry land, but the Egyptians, when they attempted to do the same, were drowned. By faith the walls of Jericho fell down after they had been encircled for seven days. By faith Rahab the prostitute did not perish with those who were disobedient, because she had given a friendly welcome to the spies. And what more shall I say? For time would fail me to tell of Gideon, Barak, Samson, Jephthah, of David and Samuel and the prophets – who through faith conquered kingdoms, enforced justice, obtained promises, stopped the mouths of lions, quenched the power of fire, escaped the edge of the sword, were made strong out of weakness, became mighty in war, put foreign armies to flight. Women received back their dead by resurrection. Some were tortured, refusing to accept release, so that they might rise again to a better life. Others suffered mocking and flogging, and even chains and imprisonment. They were stoned, they were sawn in two, they were killed with the sword. They went about in skins of sheep and goats, destitute, afflicted, mistreated – of whom the world was not worthy – wandering about in deserts and mountains, and in dens and caves of the earth. And all these, though commended through their faith, did not receive what was promised, since God had provided something better for us, that apart from us they should not be made perfect.

The faith of these people is absolutely mind-blowing! What is our excuse for faithlessness today? After all, unlike them we have Jesus, the Promise fulfilled; and we have the indwelling presence of the Holy Spirit to comfort and guide us.

---

[1] Hebrews 11:1

[2] Numbers 23:19

[3] Hebrews 13:8

[4] James 1:16-17

[5] Vine, W. E., Unger, M. F., & White, W., Jr. (1996). In *Vine's Complete Expository Dictionary of Old and New Testament Words* (Vol. 2, p. 43). T. Nelson.

[6] Ephesians 6:13

[7] Romans 12:3

[8] Matthew 6:30

[9] Matthew 8:5-10

[10] Matthew 8:26-27

[11] Mathew 15:28

[12] Matthew 17:17-18

[13] 1 Corinthians 16:13

[14] Ephesians 3:11-12

[15] Ephesians 6:16

[16] Hebrews 10:37-39

[17] 1 John 5:4

Chapter Seven:
Enduring Faith

Clearly, God is both aware of our needs and hears and answers our prayers:

> *Therefore do not be anxious, saying, 'What shall we eat?' or 'What shall we drink?' or 'What shall we wear?' For the Gentiles seek after all these things, and your heavenly Father knows that you need them all. But seek first the kingdom of God and his righteousness, and all these things will be added to you.*[1]
>
> *When he calls to me, I will answer him; I will be with him in trouble; I will rescue him and honor him.*[2]
>
> *Whatever you ask in my name, this I will do, that the Father may be glorified in the Son. If you ask me anything in my name, I will do it.*[3]

We believe Jesus' words - we believe in having faith; in fact, how many of us have asked the Lord to increase our faith? Most, if not all, of us would have to say yes. So how do we get around Jesus' reply to His disciples when they requested the same thing?

> *And Jesus answered them, "Truly, I say to you, if you have faith and do not doubt, you will not only do what has been done to the fig tree, but even if you say to this mountain, 'Be taken up and thrown into the sea,' it will happen. And whatever you ask in prayer, you will receive, if you have faith."*[4]

Now that stretches the mind! Haven't we all asked and believed for things that He's never provided? Hmmm, yep.

How can a mustard-seed sized faith move mountains, let alone bring about healing or fix a myriad of other assorted problems?

Following a conversation recently with a discouraged friend, Paul received the following insights from the Holy Spirit that help shed some light on the question:

> Faith is a legal issue. As we know it is not that you need to have 'enough' faith; but I now think that it is the **longevity of faith** that is key. When faith is maintained for a needed period of time, then the Lord God can issue an order for the Holy Ones to declare that something can now take place. **Enduring faith is key.**
>
> It seems that even just one person with enduring faith can tip the scales. It only took Abraham's faith to establish a mighty move of God.
>
> Then when I got in the Jacuzzi last night I had this thought: David had a whole heart after God, but when he was told he would be king, he did not take any advantage to make himself king, but waited until the Lord set the stage for him to become king. So is this the part of the Key of David: Isaiah 22:22 mentions double doors – two doors. Are these two doors Grace and Faith? **Grace is the Lord's part, and Faith is our part.** Two doors – grace and faith.
>
> We are now in the stage of enduring faith. Only the Lord knows how long this faith needs to be sustained in order for the Elohim-created laws to be fulfilled so that He can act according to His laws and negate what the enemy does and fulfill His, the Lord's, will.

Some may ask, "What do Holy Ones have to do with administering God's orders?" Daniel provides further insight:

> *"I saw in the visions of my head as I lay in bed, and behold, a watcher, a holy one, came down from heaven…The sentence is by the decree of the watchers, the decision by the word of the holy ones, to the end that the living may know that the Most High rules the kingdom of men and gives it to whom he will and sets over it the lowliest of men.'"* [5]
>
> *Then I heard a holy one speaking; and another holy one said to that <u>certain</u> one who was speaking.* [6]

That word, 'certain' in Hebrew is *palmoni,* and *palmoni* is a holy one, or a watcher. Some time ago, the Lord told us that the holy ones are the judicial branch of the divine government, and as it is in the physical realm, the other two branches are executive and legislative. We believe that the watchers are the police force of the judicial branch; here on earth we might call them marshals, such as are present when one goes to court. As in the physical, it seems true that the holy ones/marshals of the heavenlies are involved in making declarations and carrying out the court's orders.

In other words, if we practice enduring faith, no matter how long it takes to see God move; we can expect to eventually witness the fulfillment of His promises. Sometimes the Lord's moves are immediate and sometimes they happen during our lifetime, and sometimes it happens after we've gone. Looking first at biblical examples of faith fulfilled:

- Samuel's mother, Hannah was barren for "years and years": *For this child I prayed, and the LORD has granted me my petition that I made to him. Therefore I have lent him to the* LORD. *As long as he lives, he is lent to the* LORD." *And he worshiped the* LORD *there.*[7]

- David was extremely distressed when he and his men returned to Ziklag, only to discover that in their absence the Amalekites had captured and burned down the city, taking all of the women captive in the process. *And David inquired of the* LORD, *"Shall I pursue after this band? Shall I overtake them?" He answered him, "Pursue, for you shall surely overtake and shall surely rescue."*[8] Not only were David's wives and all of the women rescued, but his men also defeated and plundered their enemy.

- *Now there was a man in Jerusalem, whose name was Simeon, and this man was righteous and devout, waiting for the consolation of Israel, and the Holy Spirit was upon him. And it had been revealed to him by the Holy Spirit that he would not see death before he had seen the Lord's Christ. And he came in the Spirit into the temple, and when the parents brought in the child Jesus, to do for him according to the custom of the Law, he took him up in his arms and blessed God and said, "Lord, now you are letting your servant depart in peace, according to your word; for my eyes have seen your salvation that you have prepared in the presence of all peoples, a light for revelation to the Gentiles, and for glory to your people Israel."*[9]

- All of the Old Testament prophets looked forward to the arrival of the Messiah, yet none of them lived to see it in person. Did they give up on God? No. They believed in the Promise, and eventually it was fulfilled.

- The first century Church expected the imminent return of Jesus:

- Besides this you know the time, that the hour has come for you to wake from sleep. For salvation is nearer to us now than when we first believed.[10]

- The end of all things is at hand; therefore be self-controlled and sober-minded for the sake of your prayers. Above all, keep loving one another earnestly, since love covers a multitude of sins.[11]

- Children, it is the last hour, and as you have heard that antichrist is coming, so now many antichrists have come. Therefore we know that it is the last hour.[12]

Nothing has changed between biblical times and now in terms of whether God's promises are fast or slow in coming, and examples of each abound. Ultimately, we have a choice: We can choose to doubt God's promises, and give up too soon like the Israelites:

> *Then they despised the pleasant land, having no faith in his promise. They murmured in their tents, and did not obey the voice of the LORD. Therefore he raised his hand and swore to them that he would make them fall in the wilderness, and would make their offspring fall among the nations, scattering them among the lands.* [13]

Or, we can follow the many examples of the members of the Faith Hall of Fame[14] and trust that God means what He says and will always fulfill His promises:

> *Blessed is he whose help is the God of Jacob, whose hope is in the LORD his God, who made heaven and earth, the sea, and all that is in them, who keeps faith forever; who executes justice for the oppressed, who gives food to the hungry.*[15]

Enduring faith is that which carries us through the worst that the enemy can throw at us, and was not confined to Old Testament faith warriors. It manifested in New Testament times as Christians chose to die in the Roman Coliseum, and it manifested in the lives of Stephen and all of the apostles as they chose persecution and death over denouncing their faith. The apostle Paul wrote:

> *For to me to live is Christ, and to die is gain.*[16]

Moving on down through the years, enduring faith continues to be historically evident in the lives of God's people. One shining example is evident in the life of Horatio Gates Spafford, whose name most people won't recognize immediately. One year after losing his four-year-old son to scarlet fever, he and his wife and four daughters endured the massive Chicago fire in 1871. Despite their own heavy financial losses, they sought to demonstrate Christ's love by assisting other desperately hurting people. His story continues:

> In late 1873 Spafford and his wife and four daughters scheduled a trip from the United States to France. Due to work requirements, Spafford sent the rest of his family ahead of himself, aboard the French liner *Ville du Havre*. He would join them in France a few days later. On November 22, in the middle of the Atlantic, the French liner collided with the English vessel *Lochearn* and sank in twelve minutes. All four of Spafford's daughters perished; only his wife survived. She cabled him the news "Saved alone" from Wales. He quickly departed on the next ship to meet her there. When Spafford's ship passed over the spot in the High Atlantic where his daughters had succumbed to the depths, he began to pen the words "When peace like a river

attendeth my way, when sorrows like sea billows roll…" The text of the refrain is a paraphrase of the words of Julian of Norwich: "And all shall be well, and all shall be well, and all manner of things shall be well."

It required an enormous amount of faith and trust for Spafford to declare *"It Is Well with My Soul"* in the midst of such tragic loss. Yet, when we are reminded of the love of God from which nothing can separate us (Romans 8:38-39), we too can be strengthened and comforted.[17]

While we may not have recognized Spafford's name, most of us have been touched by his song, which testifies to his enduring faith:

> When peace like a river attendeth my way,
> when sorrows life sea billows roll;
> whatever my lot, thou hast taught me so say,
> "It is well, it is well with my soul"[18]

Which will we choose, a temporary faith that falls apart when bad things happen, or enduring faith that cannot be shaken? Our reactions when the enemy throws everything in his arsenal at us will tell that tale. When temporary faith is in place, doubt sets in and we begin to ask questions such as:

- Where was God when I needed Him?

- How could a loving God allow this, that or whatever?

- Why doesn't God answer my prayers?

- Why haven't God-given prophetic words or dreams been fulfilled in my life?

Temporary faith is likely to give up on God, at least some of the time, while enduring faith is rock solid because it's built on the Rock that can't be shaken. In Jesus' words:

> *"Everyone then who hears these words of mine and does them will be like a wise man who built his house on the rock. And the rain fell, and the floods came, and the winds blew and beat on that house, but it did not fall, because it had been founded on the rock. And everyone who hears these words of mine and does not do them will be like a foolish man who built his house on the sand. And the rain fell, and the floods came, and the winds blew and beat against that house, and it fell, and great was the fall of it."* [19]

Jesus was well aware that not all of us would choose wisely, as is evident in His question:

> *Nevertheless, when the Son of Man comes, will he find faith on earth?"*

Each of us has a choice to either continue on with the perception that we need more faith or to simply step into and use the mustard-sized faith we have been given. The real question then becomes whether or not our faith will be temporary or enduring.

---

[1] Matthew 6:31-33

[2] Psalm 91:15

[3] John 14:13-14

[4] Matthew 21:21-22

[5] Daniel 4:13,17

[6] Daniel 8:13.

[7] Samuel 1:27-28

[8] 1 Samuel 30:8

[9] Luke 2:25-32

[10] Romans 13:11

[11] 1 Peter 4:7

[12] 1 John2:18

[13] Psalm 106:24-27

[14] Hebrews 11

[15] Psalm 146:5-7

[16] Philippians 1:21

[17] https://bspc.org/it-is-well-with-my-soul-the-story-behind-the-hymn/

[18] https://hymnary.org/text/when_peace_like_a_river_attendeth_my_way

[19] Matthew 7:24-27

Chapter Eight:
A Hope That Endures

On June 12, 2021, I awoke with a twilight thought; something to the effect that hope is more successful, or maybe easier, when it's shared. In a dream I'd just experienced a situation that I couldn't recall, but had returned to a place that may have been my home to find a man I knew sitting on the patio. He said something about hope, to which I replied that I had been able to hold onto hope because of him. Now awake, it was clear that the man was Jesus, and I heard the hymn lyrics, "My hope is built on nothing less than Jesus' blood and righteousness…" It seemed important to look at some verses about hope:

> *And not only the creation, but we ourselves, who have the firstfruits of the Spirit, groan inwardly as we wait eagerly for adoption as sons, the redemption of our bodies. For in this hope we were saved. Now hope that is seen is not hope. For who hopes for what he sees? But if we hope for what we do not see, we wait for it with patience.* [1]

> *He delivered us from such a deadly peril, and he will deliver us. On him we have set our hope that he will deliver us again.* [2]

> *For through the Spirit, by faith, we ourselves eagerly wait for the hope of righteousness.* [3]

> *…remember that you were at that time separated from Christ, alienated from the commonwealth of Israel and strangers to the covenants of promise, having no hope and without God in the world.* [4]

Clearly, there is no hope without Jesus; all hope is worthless except in Him, so the words in the twilight moment resonated because He is the One with whom I share my hope; He is the Hope of the World; but while on earth, He placed His hope in the Father.

As Jesus' hope was strengthened by intimacy with the Father, so is mine strengthen by intimacy with the Lord; it is made possible by Jesus, strengthened by Father, and empowered by Holy Spirit through faith, which in itself is a fruit of the Spirit

The more I talk with/share my hope with the Lord, the easier/stronger/more successful I am holding onto it:

> *Now faith is the assurance of things hoped for, the conviction of things not seen.* [5]

I cling to a steadfast faith, which proclaims that God is sufficient through every circumstance. I try to live it; I write about it; I teach about it; but I also recognize that it's only possible because it is a spiritual gift that empowers me to keep on keeping on.

The Bible is full of faith stories, not the least of which is the summary account of the Old Testament saints in Hebrews 11, often referred to as the Hebrews Hall of Fame. Like them time and again, our faith is challenged; yet we are encouraged through God's Word:

> *Therefore take up the whole armor of God, that you may be able to withstand in the evil day, and having done all, to stand firm.* [6]

I must admit, life often makes it awfully difficult to keep standing!, Whether it's something like the not-so-distant Covid experience, other health issues, political unrest, or rampant injustice and unrighteousness in our society, many of us may have felt trapped in the sludge of hopelessness and despair. Perhaps our sense of peace and rest has been threatened, or has even disappeared. Where is God now? The cry of our hearts may have become that of the psalmist:

Why are you cast down O my soul, and why are you in turmoil within me?[7]

It's a verse that's repeated three times in Psalm 42 and 43; but wait - there's more, because as soon as the question is asked, the psalmist continues:

Hope in God; for I shall again praise Him, my salvation and my God.

Often, while we agree in our heart, our soul doesn't necessarily feel it. Our spirit knows without a doubt that we can rest in all of God's promises; but holding onto hope may remain a struggle when all we want to do is escape the physical reality of everyday life. Yes, we hold on tightly to our faith, but there are still the questions that countless other believers have asked down through the centuries. For example:

Why did you bring me out from the womb? Would that I had died before any eye had seen me and were as though I had not been, carried from the womb to the grave.[8]

Why, O Lord, do you stand far away? Why do you hide yourself in times of trouble?[9]

How long, O Lord? Will you forget me forever? How long will you hide your face from me? How long must I take counsel in my soul and have sorrow in my heart all the day? How long shall my enemy be exalted over me?[10]

Why do you forget us forever, why do you forsake us for so many days? [11]

During such a time of longing, I awoke one morning after a night of blessed sleep and everything suddenly seemed different. Why? While journaling, I had the thought to do a Logos search of the word, 'hope', and was astounded that the very first scripture that popped up was:

The war horse is a false hope for salvation, and by its great might it cannot rescue. [12]

That reminder really grabbed my attention! We cannot hope in any person, place or thing aside from God. Even when the plans of man are inspired by God and led by the Spirit, He must always be our ultimate source of hope; for a God-given strategy can easily fail when derailed by a bit of self-will, pride or sin of any. Psalm 33 continues:

Behold, the eye of the Lord is on those who fear him, on those who hope in his steadfast love, that he may deliver their soul from death and keep them alive in famine. Our soul waits for the Lord; he is our help and our shield. For our heart is glad in him, because we trust in his holy name. Let your steadfast love, O Lord, be upon us, even as we hope in you.

As evil swirls across our land and around the world, what better scripture could there be for the present physical reality? Has there ever been a time closer in history to the second coming of the Lord, that Day for which we all hope? No, if only because with each day that passes His return draws nearer; but however long He tarries, it appears more and more imminent as we encounter all of the things of which Jesus warned in Matthew 24. Fear of such end-times threats as well, not to mention every other obstacle the enemy can throw at us, threatens our peace on a daily basis.

All too often though, waiting and patiently trusting Him flies in the face of our desire for quick action; His mysterious ways that frequently seem so slow can challenge our faith. However:

> *The Lord is not slow to fulfill his promise as some count slowness, but is patient toward you, not wishing that any should perish, but that all should reach repentance.*[13]

You see, hope is the expectation of the future attainment of a desired object or outcome. It is often associated with trust, whether in God or others.

> In Hebrew, hope is expressed most commonly with the verbs קָוָה (*qāwâ*, "to wait") and יָחַל (*yāḥal*, "to wait") and nouns related to these. The verb *qāwâ* conveys a sense of waiting with expectation.[14]

Get that? I suppose I've known that hope involves waiting, but haven't put them together in such close proximity. Essentially, hope requires waiting, for a hope that has been fulfilled no longer requires waiting for it to happen. Hope is made evident in the waiting; the two go hand-in-hand. Consider this familiar verse:

> *So now faith, hope, and love abide, these three; but the greatest of these is love.*[15]

Researching hope in Logos , I read (bold text mine):

> Hope, it would seem, is a psychological necessity, if man is to envisage the future at all. Even if there are no rational grounds for it, man still continues to hope. Very naturally such hope, even when it

appears to be justified, is transient and illusory; and it is remarkable how often it is qualified by poets and other writers by such epithets as 'faint', 'trembling', 'feeble', 'desperate', 'phantom'. The Bible sometimes uses hope in the conventional sense. The ploughman, for example, should plough in hope (1 Cor. 9:10), for it is the hope of reward that sweetens labour. But for the most part the hope with which the Bible is concerned is something very different; and in comparison with it, other hope is scarcely recognized as hope. The majority of secular thinkers in the ancient world did not regard hope as a virtue, but merely as a temporary illusion; and Paul was giving an accurate description of pagans when he said they had no hope (Eph. 2:12; *cf.* 1 Thes. 4:13), the fundamental reason for this being that they were 'without God'.

Where there is a belief in the living God, who acts and intervenes in human life and who can be trusted to implement his promises, hope in the specifically biblical sense becomes possible. Such hope is not a matter of temperament, nor is it conditioned by prevailing circumstances or any human possibilities. It does not depend upon what a man possesses, upon what he may be able to do for himself, nor upon what any other human being may do for him… **Biblical hope is inseparable therefore from faith in God.** Because of what God has done in the past, particularly in preparing for the coming of Christ, and because of what God has done and is now doing through Christ, the Christian dares to expect future blessings at present invisible (2 Cor. 1:10)… [therefore] it is not surprising that hope should so often be mentioned as a concomitant of faith…**What is perhaps more remarkable is the frequent association of hope with love as well as with faith. This threefold combination of faith, hope and love is found in 1 Thes. 1:3; 5:8; Gal. 5:5-6; 1 Cor. 13:13; Heb. 6:10-12; 1 Pet. 1:21-22**. By its connection with love, Christian hope is freed from all selfishness… **Faith, hope and love are thus inseparable. Hope cannot exist apart from faith, and love cannot be exercised without hope. These three are the things that abide (1 Cor. 13:13) and together they comprise the Christian way of life.**[16]

Looking back anew at any why-are-you-cast-down-O-my-soul complaint in Psalm 42-43, the Lord ties it all together in one verse:

> *By day the Lord commands his steadfast love, and at night his song is with me, a prayer to the God of my life.*[17]

It is His steadfast love that makes it possible for us to enter into faith, hope and love, and in alignment with His truth, we can proclaim:

> *But this I call to mind, and therefore I have hope: The steadfast love of the Lord never ceases; his mercies never come to an end; they are new every morning; great is your faithfulness. "The Lord is my portion," says my soul, "therefore I will hope in him."*[18]

Perseverance, counting the cost, waiting on the Lord, living by faith and enduring; all are directly connected to a hope that will not disappoint:

> *Therefore, since we have been justified by faith, we have peace with God through our Lord Jesus Christ. Through him we have also obtained access by faith into this grace*

in which we stand, and we rejoice in hope of the glory of God. Not only that, but we rejoice in our sufferings, knowing that suffering produces endurance, and endurance produces character, and character produces hope, and hope does not put us to shame, because God's love has been poured into our hearts through the Holy Spirit who has been given to us.[19]

---

[1] Romans 8:23-25

[2] 2 Corinthians 1:10

[3] Galatians 5:5

[4] Ephesians 2:12

[5] Hebrews 11:1

[6] Ephesians 6:13

[7] Psalm 42:5

[8] Job 10:18-19

[9] Psalm 10:1

[10] Psalm 13:1-2

[11] Lamentations 5:20

[12] Psalm 33:17

[13] 2 Peter 3:9

[14] Fenlason, A. C. (2014). Hope. D. Mangum, D. R. Brown, R. Klippenstein, & R. Hurst (Eds.), *Lexham Theological Wordbook*. Bellingham, WA: Lexham Press.

[15] 1 Corinthians 13:13

[16] Tasker, R. V. G. (1996). Hope. In D. R. W. Wood, I. H. Marshall, A. R. Millard, J. I. Packer, & D. J. Wiseman (Eds.), *New Bible dictionary* (3rd ed., pp. 479-480). Leicester, England; Downers Grove, IL: InterVarsity Press.

[17] Psalm 42:8

[18] Lamentations 3:21-24

[19] Romans 5:1-5

Chapter Nine:
Entering the Rest

Barbara's note: As the Lord began speaking about the development of this book, it soon became obvious that His Rest was to be an important component. But haven't we written about that before? I searched through all of our books and realized that no, we haven't. For years, we've both talked about it and experienced it often, but it seems God also wanted the article Paul wrote years ago to be included as part of this discussion.

Entering the Rest of the Lord:
Our travels have taken us to many countries around the world and we have not only met many wonderful people, but have also observed God working in higher and higher degrees of power. Yet, regardless of the many different cultures and languages, we have enjoyed similar experiences in each location; for in each seminar God has always perfectly provided just the right church, worship team and intercessors. Invariably, everything has worked out well.

But another aspect of our ministry is that we sit down with people on an individual basis and hear their stories. We listen to accounts of not being wanted before birth, of rotten childhoods, of marriages that have been devastated; horrible stories from normal people.

We have often heard from people who, upon reaching their fifties and sixties, have realized that the great dreams and the great prophecies that have been spoken over them have not yet been fulfilled. They wonder if anything is ever going to change. It seems like they're always receiving healing, but are never being completely healed.

One day during a ministry session at Aslan's Place, a lady in her fifties shared another very, very sad story. Relationships had not worked out, children had not come, she was miserable in church, she was miserable at work, and she had been a Christian for decades. As I listened to her I was reminded of the play, *Les Miserables*, which is the story of a man named Valjean, a prisoner who was taken in by a priest following his release. The morning after entering the priest's home, breakfast was served and, as the priest left the room, Valjean grabbed a candlestick and ran. After the police caught him and brought him back they inquired, "Is this the man who was at your house, and did he steal this candlestick?" The priest replied, "No, he didn't steal it, I gave it to him. In fact I gave him both but he forgot to take the other one." And so, Valjean left, experiencing the grace and forgiveness of Jesus Christ for the first time, and that very grace and forgiveness is the underlying theme of the entire play.

Eventually, Valjean became a very important man. He started helping people and even became the mayor of a city., eventually meeting a woman named Fantine and her daughter, Cosette. Very early in the play, when Fantine realized that she would soon die and leave Cosette as an orphan, she sings a song called *I Dreamed a Dream:*

> There was a time when men were kind
> When their voices were soft
> And their words inviting
> There was a time when love was blind
> And the world was a song
> And the song was exciting

In the Midst of the Storm: Stillness

There was a time
Then it all went wrong

I dreamed a dream in time gone by
When hope was high
And life worth living
I dreamed that love would never die
I dreamed that God would be forgiving
Then I was young and unafraid
And dreams were made and used and wasted
There was no ransom to be paid
No song unsung, no wine untasted

But the tigers come at night
With their voices soft as thunder
As they tear your hope apart
And they turn your dream to shame

He slept a summer by my side
He filled my days with endless wonder
He took my childhood in his stride
But he was gone when autumn came

And still I dream he'll come to me
That we will live the years together
But there are dreams that cannot be
And there are storms we cannot weather

I had a dream my life would be
So different from this hell I'm living
So different now from what it seemed
Now life has killed the dream I dreamed

As I ministered to that woman, I recalled that song; so I played the CD for her. She wept as she realized that the song seemed to be an account of her own life. But it's not just her life; it easily describes the lives of many people, for we all dream dreams. We all believe that things are going to get better but they don't, and many of us have heard so many unfulfilled prophetic words that we have wondered, "When is anything good going to happen to me? When is ministry going to start happening for me? When am I going to find a place in a church where I am going to be accepted?" Pretty soon, we find that life has killed our dreams. It's a sad fact the Church is filled with people who have silently dreamed dreams but have been disappointed by life. Unfortunately our churches, the very places we would expect to receive comfort, are not always very understanding. All too often they do not comprehend that the Church is filled with hurting people who are afraid to let anybody know because they fear further rejection or disappointment.

We may have had an unhappy childhood and, as a teenager, thought, "If I can just move out, if I can just be free of my parents, then everything will be okay." So we moved out, but thirty days later the bills started coming and we were surprised because now someone expected that we were going to pay for those bills.

Or, perhaps we've dreamed that if we would get married then everything would be okay, so we got married. Then we thought, "If I have children, then it will be better," so we had children; and after three or four nights of not sleeping we thought, "Well, I need to buy a house," so we bought a house and it had to be repaired. Then we bought toys, adult toys, and they needed to be repaired too.

We also have dreams of what the church should be, what our pastor should be, what our friends should be; and we seem to be crushed by disappointment continually when things don't turn out the way we thought they should. And so we wonder, "Is this what life is really about?"

I remember watching a cartoon with our children. A little mouse escaped with his father out of a room, only to fall into a trash can. The little mouse asked its dad, "Is this what the world is like?" Sadly, we've come to think that is what the world is like; we believe any little success must certainly be followed by a larger failure.

I had the wonderful opportunity of hearing Dean Sherman of Youth With a Mission very early in our training in spiritual warfare. He made this comment, "If you look at all of entertainment, it rotates around three things; a great romance, a great adventure, or a great conflict." Such a helpful insight, for we in the Church are involved in the greatest conflict in the universe; we are involved in the greatest adventure in the universe; and we are involved in the greatest romance in the universe. So yes, we can expect something to be different in our lives.

In our meetings we have found that oftentimes when the Lord wants to do something special with us - something involving great romance, adventure, and conflict - the cherubim have shown up. I once delivered this message to a group of five American Baptist churches in the San Diego area, and God came in great power. My pastor-friend, Brian Fairley, said, "Paul, they were doing really good until you said, 'The cherubim are here.'" I replied, "Well, they are in the Bible;" and he answered, "I know, but it freaked them out." So, let's look at what the cherubim are.

Cherubim are mentioned in three places in the Bible, Ezekiel 1, Ezekiel 10, and Revelation 4:

> *As I looked, behold, a stormy wind came out of the north, and a great cloud, with brightness around it, and fire flashing forth continually, and in the midst of the fire, as it were gleaming metal. And from the midst of it came the likeness of four living creatures. And this was their appearance: they had a human likeness, but each had four faces, and each of them had four wings. Their legs were straight, and the soles of their feet were like the sole of a calf's foot. And they sparkled like burnished bronze.* [1]

These four living creatures are identified as cherubim in Ezekiel 10, and they are in the pillar of fire, which is in the cloud of His glory. Continuing with verses 8-17,:

> *Under their wings on their four sides they had human hands. And the four had their faces and their wings thus: their wings touched one another. Each one of them went straight forward, without turning as they went. As for the likeness of their faces, each had a human face. The four had the face of a lion on the right side, the four had the face of an ox on the left side, and the four had the face of an eagle. Such were their faces. And their wings were spread out above. Each creature had two wings, each of which touched the wing of another, while two covered their bodies. And each went straight forward. Wherever the spirit would go, they went, without turning as they went. As for the likeness of the living creatures, their appearance was like burning coals of fire, like the appearance of torches moving to and fro among the living creatures. And the fire was bright, and out of the fire went forth lightning. And the living creatures darted to and fro, like the appearance of a flash of lightning. Now as I looked at the living creatures, I saw a wheel on the earth beside the living creatures, one for each of the four of them. As for the appearance of the wheels and their construction: their appearance was like the gleaming of*

> beryl. And the four had the same likeness, their appearance and construction being as it were a wheel within a wheel. When they went, they went in any of their four directions without turning as they went.

Visualize the four of them, somehow all going forward and moving together in unity with, as we are told later, the fire in their feet. I believe this is where the anointing that we can discern is sent from. Of course, the anointing actually comes from the Holy Spirit, but it appears that the living creatures have the fire between their feet, which sometimes hits us as we worship. It also can appear as lightning, and is pretty spectacular! Verse 18:

> And their rims were tall and awesome, and the rims of all four were full of eyes all around.

Now, you do not go outside and look at an automobile wheel and say, "Oh, what an awesome wheel that is. Right? Awesome means big - really big - maybe as big as a large room; now, that's awesome! And can you imagine all of those eyes blinking? Isn't that weird? It would definitely make for a good video game! Verses 19-20:

> And when the living creatures went, the wheels went beside them; and when the living creatures rose from the earth, the wheels rose. Wherever the spirit wanted to go, they went, and the wheels rose along with them, for the spirit of the living creatures was in the wheels.

So now we have been told two things; wherever the Spirit of God goes the cherubim go and their spirits are in the wheels. They are living wheels. Verses 21-22:

> When those went, these went; and when those stood, these stood; and when those rose from the earth, the wheels rose along with them, for the spirit of the living

> *creatures was in the wheels. Over the heads of the living creatures there was the likeness of an expanse, shining like awe-inspiring crystal, spread out above their heads.*

Above the heads of these four living creatures is the crystal sea. It does not say the crystal pond; it does not say the crystal lake; it says the crystal sea. What is the nature of a sea? When you stand on a sea coast, you look and cannot see the end of the sea because it is too big. So, these four are not six feet tall; they are BIG. I believe they would appear as thousands of feet high if we were able to see them in the physical reality of our third dimension, and they are holding the crystal sea. Verses 23-24:

> *And under the expanse their wings were stretched out straight, one toward another. And each creature had two wings covering its body. And when they went, I heard the sound of their wings like the sound of many waters, like the sound of the Almighty, a sound of tumult like the sound of an army. When they stood still, they let down their wings.*

There they are, flapping their wings; and their wings alone must be really big. Have you ever seen those old Roman movies where you have ten million soldiers going down a hillside and there are ten million voices that make a loud noise. Have you ever stood by Niagara Falls? Very, very noisy! This is like the noise of their wings; this is not like the buzz of a housefly. Verse 26a:

> *And above the expanse over their heads there was the likeness of a throne, in appearance like sapphire...*

So, in addition to the cloud, the pillar of fire with the four living creatures in it and the crystal sea, we now have a throne; and this is really huge. I've learned, thanks to a man in Minnesota who heard this message, that the nature of a sapphire stone when light goes into it is intensified twelve times, and then it goes out in many directions. Verses 26b-28:

> ...and seated above the likeness of a throne was a likeness with a human appearance. And upward from what had the appearance of his waist I saw as it were gleaming metal, like the appearance of fire enclosed all around. And downward from what had the appearance of his waist I saw as it were the appearance of fire, and there was brightness around him. Like the appearance of the bow that is in the cloud on the day of rain, so was the appearance of the brightness all around. Such was the appearance of the likeness of the glory of the LORD. And when I saw it, I fell on my face, and I heard the voice of one speaking.

I cannot understand this. His glory, His light, is coming off of Him; it is as intense as is possible, and His eternal, everlasting greatness is magnified a dozen times bigger, literally coming out as laser beams. This is very important because we are told that the Hebrew translation of the glory that came off Moses is that his face shot forth beams of light. He was, 'laser faced'.

So what happens when the cherubim show up? Three things. First, there is movement:

> And he said to me, "Son of man, stand on your feet, and I will speak with you."

We are told in Ezekiel 10, that the spirit came into Ezekiel and actually moved him away from where he was to a different place. You see, when the cherubim show up, the glory of God is present; and when the glory of God is present, there is movement. We are moved from where we are to where we need to be in our lives, in our marriages, in our family, in our ministry, in our motivations and in every single area of life. Because there is movement, we are taken from where we are to where we need to be.

Second, there is a message. In Ezekiel 3, a message was delivered in a scroll; and third, there is a ministry. Ezekiel was told to go and speak God's words.

The cherubim do not show up in our meetings just so we can talk about them; there is always something more that is going on. There is movement; there is a message; there is a ministry.

In December of 1999, it was a great privilege when we were called to go and minister at the Toronto Airport Church. Before we left, John Arnott called and asked if I would preach in the Sunday evening service to conclude our week there, which was terrifying enough. Then, after a couple of days they said they would like for us to speak at the Spanish church on Sunday morning, which would be translated live, and I thought that would be OK. But finally, a few days later, John Arnott called once more and said they were going to combine the English and Spanish church and they would like for me to preach to them all on Sunday morning. That was enough to terrify me totally.

I had a sermon prepared that I felt like God had matured in me about the Glory of God. Very early in my Baptist days I'd been preaching through the book of Exodus when I came to the passage where Moses said, "Lord, show me Your glory." The reason he'd said that was because God was angry at the people after He looked down and saw them sacrificing to idols; in fact, they were sacrificing their children. Not just sacrifices of grain and fruit; in that culture you sacrificed babies, which was exactly what they were doing and God basically said to Moses, "I want you to go down and deal with that."

So Moses went down the mountain and he saw it too, becoming very angry. Then he and God had this talk: God said, "Now, Moses what are you going to do with your people?" And Moses answered, "They are not my people, they are Your people." God then replied, "Well, I'm just going to wipe them out." So Moses argued, "God, you can't do that. What is going to happen to Your Name, to Your fame? What are people going to think about You? Are they going to say, 'You're the kind of God that brings somebody out of Egypt and then You kill them all?'"

So, Moses contended with God; he laid ahold of God, and God was not budging until finally Moses went for the ultimate prayer, "Lord, show me Your glory." So I preached on this; and right about now you're probably thinking, "What does that have to do with what we have just been talking about?" Read on.

The Lord answered immediately, "Yes, I will show you My glory;" and He put Moses in the cleft of the rock as His glory passed by. Then He started proclaiming His name, and the meaning within His name is "I am a God who forgives and has everlasting patience." So Moses said, "See, I told You. That is Your name, and I am claiming that." So God promised, "I will go with You and I will keep the covenant."

That's the message I preached in Toronto. Now, if there is any place where the fire could fall, it was Toronto. You could sneeze and lay out half the people. When I got to the end and said, "Lord, release Your glory," I was waiting for the fireworks, but what happened was not at all what I expected. There was a little pause, and people started shaking; then people all over the place started lying down on the floor. The Toronto church has a huge front area that is empty, plus adjoining aisles, and pretty soon there were over 1000 people who were all lying down everywhere, and it got really quiet. I thought, "I have put people to sleep with my sermons before but I have never been this effective!" So I finally just sat down next to John and said, "Okay John, I think I'm done," and he just looked at me and didn't even say anything; so I just sat there for 15 or 20 minutes with nothing going on. You just can't do that in church. You have to have something going on!

I went home and prayed, "Lord, every other time I have done this Your fire has come, and the anointing has come, and we've prayed for people and they'd go flying, and we'd just have a wonderful time. What is this?"

Sometime later, I was impacted by a prophecy I received that had been dated January 4, 2002. It was by Mike McClung and was titled, *2002 A Year of Rest, Preparation and Breakthrough*:

> 2002 a year of rest, preparation, and breakthrough. 2002 will begin the entering of the Sabbath rest. The true lordship of Christ and His resurrection glory is about to be revealed in a most profound manner to those who have pursued intimacy with Him. We now understand that Christ Himself is our Sabbath and we are to labor to enter into the fullness of His presence and rest. There is a great wave of healing and deliverance coming to the Church for the purpose of healing the wounded body of Christ, releasing the harvest. One problem that will rise is that religious people will become very angry and embittered towards those who are pursuing Him in rest. In entering His rest there will be unlimited

provision, unlimited love and intimacy, unlimited authority, and unlimited opportunity. We will begin to see Him and the beauty of His riches, His resurrection glory and holiness, and no longer just as He is presented in the gospels in His poverty as the lowly servant. The shekinah cloud of His presence will be seen resting in places and geographical regions around the world. This will prepare us to come into intimate oneness with Him and His purpose and to be trusted with greater anointing, authority, and responsibility.

Next, I was in the San Jose area and I was doing deliverance for a lady. There were five of us present and as I began, out of my mouth came these words, "Now, you need to understand, I did not plan to say these things. You understand this don't you? Lord, take us to the fourth dimension for this deliverance." All of a sudden, it was like we were in an elevator and started going up. The power of God hit this woman and she started shaking, so we all just sat there while the Lord did deliverance on her. I wasn't needed any more, so I was looking around trying to decide what I was supposed to do, and I had the thought, "Paul, try to worry about something right now."

I must tell you that I could have received the gold medal for worry in my life. I was a great worrier, not a warrior, a worrier; and I could worry with the best of them. I'm sure I could surpass you at any level, and I had some big things to worry about too. You know you're alive if you have things to worry about.

So there I was, trying to worry, but I couldn't! I thought, "What is this place?" So I said to the other four people, "Try to worry right now." They started laughing and said, "We can't worry." We had gone to another place.

I want you to follow me now: The Bible says we are seated with Christ in heavenly places, not in a place. The scientific and mathematical names for those places are dimensions, and that is biblical. But we are not there all the time. Positionally, we should be there, but in our soul and our spirit we are not always there.

I mentioned before that there is the cloud, the pillar, and the cherubim. I can discern all of these when they appear in one of our meetings, and when the cloud shows up and people walk through it, something happens. In Exodus 13:21 we read:

> *And the LORD went before them by day in a pillar of cloud to lead them along the way, and by night in a pillar of fire to give them light, that they might travel by day and by night.*

What happens? You follow the cloud, right? You go where the cloud leads you, and there is judgment that takes place in the cloud. We find that the cloud was behind the children of Israel, and on the other side were the people of Egypt, and judgment fell on them.

> *And the LORD said to Moses, "Behold, I am coming to you in a thick cloud, that the people may hear when I speak with you, and may also believe you forever."* [2]

There is communication when the cloud comes. We are told that the cloud came over the tent of meeting, right? It is the tent of His presence, the tent of meeting. It was there where Moses talked to the Lord. Like the Israelites, when the cloud moves, we go with it; and as we travel we go to a place where there is communication. That communication may be visual, it may be auditory, or it may be simply a knowing in one's spirit.

I want to say something very carefully; in intimacy in marriage much is said without being said. That is real intimacy. We somehow think we need to yak and talk and talk and yak to have intimacy with the Lord. But sometimes He just wants us to be with Him and experience His love.

In 2 Chronicles 5:13-14, we see that the trumpeters and the singers joined in unison as one voice to give praise and thanks to the Lord, accompanied by trumpets and cymbals and other instruments. They raised their voices, praised the Lord and sang, "He is good; His love endures forever." Then the temple of the Lord was filled with the cloud and the priests could not perform their service because the cloud of the glory of the Lord filled the temple of God. His glory is in the cloud, which is the manifest presence of His glory.

In Matthew 17:5, there is a proclamation of who Jesus is, and again there is communication as the cloud comes:

> *He was still speaking when, behold, a bright cloud overshadowed them, and a voice from the cloud said, "This is my beloved Son, with whom I am well pleased; listen to him."*

In Acts 1:9, Jesus ascended into the cloud. It's the same cloud, and one day He is going to come back in that cloud, the cloud of His shekinah glory.

What does this all mean? I want to be very practical here. When the cherubim are present, there is movement; the cloud moves and we follow it for the Lord wants to move us from where we are to where we need to be; and He wants us to enter into His rest. Apostle Paul wrote:

> *...that the God of our Lord Jesus Christ, the Father of glory, may give you the Spirit of wisdom and of revelation in the knowledge of him, having the eyes of your hearts enlightened, that you may know what is the hope to which he has called you, what are the riches of his glorious inheritance in the saints, and what is the immeasurable greatness of his power toward us who believe, according to the working of his great might that he worked in Christ when he raised him from the dead and seated him at his right hand in the heavenly places, far above all rule and authority and power and dominion, and above every name that is named, not only in this age but also in the one to come.*[3]

Apostle John wrote:

> *After this I looked, and behold, a door standing open in heaven! And the first voice, which I had heard speaking to me like a trumpet, said, "Come up here, and I will show you what must take place after this."* [4]

That is not just something that happened in the Bible; it's for us here and now. He wants us to enter into the place of rest. Let me give you some more verses:

> *And he said, "My presence will go with you, and I will give you rest."* [5]

> *And I say, "Oh, that I had wings like a dove! I would fly away and be at rest..."* [6]

> *My soul finds rest in God alone. My salvation comes from Him... Find rest oh my soul in God alone. My hope comes from Him.* [7]

> *He who dwells in the shelter of the Most High will abide in the shadow of the Almighty.*[8]

You see, not everybody dwells there. When we dwell in the place of rest, then we are told we will rest in the shadow of the Almighty, and everything is then under our feet. The enemy is only under our feet when we enter into the place of rest.

> *For thus said the Lord GOD, the Holy One of Israel, "In returning and rest you shall be saved; in quietness and in trust shall be your strength."* [9]
>
> *Thus says the LORD: "Stand by the roads, and look, and ask for the ancient paths, where the good way is; and walk in it, and find rest for your souls. But they said, 'We will not walk in it.'"* [10]
>
> *Come to me, all who labor and are heavy laden, and I will give you rest. Take my yoke upon you, and learn from me, for I am gentle and lowly in heart, and you will find rest for your souls. For my yoke is easy, and my burden is light."* [11]
>
> *Therefore, while the promise of entering his rest still stands, let us fear lest any of you should seem to have failed to reach it... So then, there remains a Sabbath rest for the people of God, for whoever has entered God's rest has also rested from his works as God did from his.* [12]

Why is it that we are so frustrated, so unhappy, and so unfulfilled in our dreams and our expectations? Why is it that we are so discontent because we have not entered into the kind of ministries that have been prophesied about us, and that we have not fulfilled the things that we have been given to accomplish? It is because we have not entered into His rest, and we are still striving and working to try to make it happen. We work, and we work, and we work; and God says to us, "Why don't you just let go of it and enter into My rest?"

God has said to us, "Now make every effort to enter into the rest." So, there is one thing we need to work at friends, and this is it: we need to work at entering His rest. Why?

I once heard Heidi Baker, and she helped me understand this because she has not only learned to enter into the rest but she also lives there. Everything happens in His rest; it's there where ideas come; it's where strategies originate; it's there where warfare takes place; it's there where ministries are birthed. It all happens in His presence, in His rest. I no longer need to plan and scheme; I do not need to start a media ministry; I do not need to try to raise money for buildings; I don't really need to do anything except go into His rest and let Him do it. It's a new way of doing Church.

God is the one who started Aslan's Place and everything that has happened significantly since the birthing of Aslan's Place, He has done. Donna and I are just trying to keep up with what He's doing. Anything we have tried to initiate or start on our own has not worked; so I am finally getting it. He wants me to be in His rest, to believe Him and to enjoy Him; even while I also enjoy my wife, my children, my grandchildren; and being with people, being in love with people and serving them. Our God is the One who will make it all happen.

I don't care whether you are a businessman or a minister, it works. I expect that there are going to be new kinds of board meetings in which a board is going to enter into His rest and let Him speak. Then they will say, "Oh my goodness, what a wonderful idea;" and they will no longer claim the credit.

Isaiah said, "Lord all that I have done, You have accomplished for me." Do you understand that every good thought, every good thing that you do is His idea first? He just lets us look good while He's working things out for good.

There are two ways that you know that you have entered His rest. As stated before, one is that it is impossible to worry; and the second is that you cannot be jealous of anyone else's gifts.

Heidi Baker has said that the pastors simply need to get down, lay on the floor and act like a bunch of dead people until they get something done in the church. So I invite you to do it; just relax in a comfortable position and enter into His rest. If you can see into spiritual realms, then look; if you can hear, listen, and you might just experience peace. Because He is God, He will take you where He wants you to be.

I was with a medical doctor and the Lord took us up into His presence. He came back later and told me, "I was sitting in a lounge chair in a place in the heavens. An angel came by like a waiter and gave me a drink with an umbrella. The angel looked at me and asked, 'Can't you ever relax?' before he handed me the drink and walked off smiling."

Enjoy His place of rest. It is the Holy of Holies, the tent of meeting, Mount Zion, the secret place, the place of intimacy, the shelter of the Most High, the tent of His presence, the mountain of the Lord, the bedchamber, God's bosom, a place of waiting. It is the higher ground.

---

[1] Ezekiel 1:4-7

[2] Exodus 19:9

[3] Ephesians 1:17-21

[4] Revelation 4:1
[5] Exodus 33:14
[6] Psalm 55:6
[7] Psalm 62:1,5 NKJV
[8] Psalm 91:1
[9] Isaiah 30:15
[10] Jeremiah 6:16
[11] Matthew 11:28-30
[12] Hebrews 4:1, 9-10

Chapter Ten:
KNOWING GOD

At this point, many may feel a bit like the rich young ruler who, though he seemed to have it all, still knew at some deep level that he was missing something. But unlike that young man most, if not all, who have reached this point in our book already have experienced the saving faith that he still lacked. Perhaps the concepts of perseverance, enduring faith, counting the cost and rest are familiar; perhaps they even sound wonderful; and yet, perhaps there's also something deep inside that is crying out for more. And that's a good place to be, for we can never have enough of God, and every one of us should be on a lifelong journey to know Him better:

> *The fear of the Lord is the beginning of wisdom, and the knowledge of the Holy One is insight.*[1]

Do you remember the lyrics from *Game of Love*, the popular oldies-but goodies tune from the sixties? "It started long ago in the Garden of Eden, when Adam said to Eve, baby you're for me?" That phrase wasn't so far off the mark:

> *Then the Lord God made a woman from the rib, and he brought her to the man. "At last!" the man exclaimed. "This one is bone from my bone, and flesh from my flesh! She will be called 'woman,' because she was taken from 'man.' "*[2]

Unfortunately, the first couple made the fateful decision to eat from the fruit of tree of the knowledge of good and evil, choosing to disobey God's perfect plan for their lives in an effort to become more like Him; and it's been all downhill from there as mankind has continued his quest to gain intellectual understanding about all that we encounter. We send our kids to the best schools and push them to study, study, and study some more. We work hard in our jobs to stay abreast of the latest developments so new technology won't render us obsolete. We become obsessed with reading, studying, taking notes and memorizing facts about the things that are of most interest to us. To be honest, that's not always a bad thing; after all, God did invent knowledge, and intellectual understanding can often be a good thing when pursued appropriately. Sadly though, the events in the Garden skewed God's concept of righteous knowledge, spinning it out of balance from His perfect plan.

> *And the Spirit of the Lord shall rest upon him, the Spirit of wisdom and understanding, the Spirit of counsel and might, the Spirit of knowledge and the fear of the Lord. And his delight shall be in the fear of the Lord.*[3]

You see; wisdom, understanding, counsel, might, knowledge and the fear of the Lord are meant to work together in conjunction with the Spirit of the Lord. They are meant to complement each other; but all too often we place knowledge at the top, constantly seeking facts and figures as we try to extrapolate wisdom and understanding from the corrupted knowledge of the world.

We do this not only in our day-to-day roles at work, home or play, but also in our pursuit of God; which is not His perfect plan. Yes, He wants us to be knowledgeable about Him, but studying everything we can find and trying to pack our brains full of such knowledge isn't the way we're going to get it. By so doing, we fall into the same trap as Adam and Eve, seeking after the tree of the knowledge of good and evil. We seem to think if we just absorb enough of this knowledge we'll have all the answers, but that never happens and can easily get so caught up in the quest to figure God out that we never get around to experiencing Him. We miss the truth:

> *For my thoughts are not your thoughts, neither are your ways my ways, declares the Lord. For as the heavens are higher than the earth, so are my ways higher than your ways and my thoughts than your thoughts.*[4]

> *Oh, the depth of the riches and wisdom and knowledge of God! How unsearchable are his judgments and how inscrutable his ways!*[5]

Wanting to know God is admirable, and we should constantly seek Him out:

> *Seek the Lord, all you humble of the land, who do his just commands; seek righteousness; seek humility; perhaps you may be hidden on the day of the anger of the Lord.*[6]

But if knowing Him isn't the same thing as having an intellectual knowledge of Him, what are we to do? One morning, the Lord woke me up and gave me a quick overview of how to know Him more intimately, and I remembered God's promise:

> *... and he will be the stability of your times, abundance of salvation, wisdom, and knowledge; the fear of the Lord is Zion's treasure.*[7]

It was very clear to me that it is His desire that we know Him well, and then I was shown five ways it can happen outside of our own pursuit of knowledge:

1) Hunger for God: Moses cried out, "Teach me your ways so I can know you." This was after he'd been up Mt. Sinai the first time and had come back down to find the people in sin, worshipping a golden calf. God's response to Moses' plea was to place him in a protected place, in the cleft of a rock as He passed by in the fullness of His glory. God called Moses His friend. Why? Because he was always hungry for more; he just couldn't get enough of His Lord.

Consider the necessity of food to sustain life: As the body approaches death, it is a very normal thing for a person to lose all desire for food or water. In fact, they eventually lose the ability to swallow anything; and even if they did, their body could no longer process it. The need for food and water is evidence of life, and if we carry the analogy over into the spiritual realm, hunger and thirst for God is what keeps us alive spiritually; it's what keeps us growing in our understanding or knowledge of Him.

> *Blessed are those who hunger and thirst for righteousness, for they shall be satisfied.*[8]

2) Intimacy with God: Just as intimate relationships between people are developed through a process of building trust and communication over time, so are the intimacies of God revealed to us. In high school, teenage girls tell secrets to girlfriends they trust; sweethearts who are dating begin sharing secrets with one another; in a good marriage, husbands and wives become even more intimate, sharing not only their hearts and minds, but also their bodies. As trust is gained, the manner in which relationships deepen reflects the manner in which we gain knowledge of God. The more time we spend with Him, the more He shares His mysteries with us.

How do we do that? Reading His Word is a start; but we must read with a listening ear for the Spirit's prompting that there is something special there for you; or perhaps reading until a particular verse just jumps off the page and burns itself into your heart. Then it will be clear that you've heard from the Lord; that He has imparted knowledge.

Praying and worshipping are helpful practices, but simply waiting quietly for Him cannot be undervalued.

> *Listen to my voice in the morning, LORD. Each morning I bring my requests to you and wait expectantly.* [9]

Then, suddenly He speaks and you have a new understanding of something; or, you may actually hear his voice. You will have found knowledge through intimacy.

> *Your word is a lamp to my feet and a light to my path.* [10]

3) Experiential knowledge: God is gracious in that even when we aren't willing to hungrily seek after Him, He shows Himself in other ways. We experience His intervention on our behalf; we experience His hand and His power at work in our lives.

> *Say therefore to the people of Israel, 'I am the Lord, and I will bring you out from under the burdens of the Egyptians, and I will deliver you from slavery to them, and I will redeem you with an outstretched arm and with great acts of judgment. I will take you to be my people, and I will be your God, and you shall know that I am the Lord your God, who has brought you out from under the burdens of the Egyptians.* [11]

How many times has God delivered each one of us from a difficult, seemingly hopeless situation? Perhaps it was financial or relational, or perhaps an illness that had no solution aside from God's intervention. Such times, whether we recognized it or not, were opportunities to know Him better, to know His love, His power; to gain that elusive knowledge that cannot be found in books.

> *I sought the LORD, and he answered me and delivered me from all my fears. Those who look to him are radiant, and their faces shall never be ashamed. This poor man cried, and the LORD heard him and saved him out of all his troubles.*[12]

4) Observation: All we have to do is open our eyes – open our hearts – and observe God's Hand at work in the lives of mankind to gain knowledge of Him. He's not out of the miracle working business either, so watch and see what the Lord can do:

> *And the Egyptians shall know that I am the Lord, when I have gotten glory over Pharaoh, his chariots, and his horsemen."* [13]

> *But Jesus, knowing their thoughts, said, "Why do you think evil in your hearts? For which is easier, to say, 'Your sins are forgiven,' or to say, 'Rise and walk'? But that you may know that the Son of Man has authority on earth to forgive sins" – he then said to the paralytic – "Rise, pick up your bed and go home."* [14]

Well, some may say, that's fine for the ancient Egyptians and the people of Jesus day, but when do we have the chance to observe such things? Scripture is clear that His works surround us daily:

> *For the wrath of God is revealed from heaven against all ungodliness and unrighteousness of men, who by their unrighteousness suppress the truth. For what can be known about God is plain to them, because God has shown it to them. For his invisible attributes, namely, his eternal power and divine nature, have been clearly perceived, ever since the creation of the world, in the things that have been made. So they are without excuse.*[15]

Did you notice that last sentence? *So they are without excuse.* When we stand before God, we will be left with zero justification for not knowing Him!!!

5) Judgment: All men everywhere will eventually have a sure and certain knowledge of the true and living God! Surely this is not the way we would choose to know Him:

> *And they will be loathsome in their own sight for the evils that they have committed, for all their abominations. And they shall know that I am the Lord. I have not said in vain that I would do this evil to them."* [16]

How much better to learn of Him now, and to experience all of God's blessings than to gain experiential knowledge of His wrath once it's too late:

> *For God says, "At just the right time, I heard you. On the day of salvation, I helped you." Indeed, the "right time" is now. Today is the day of salvation.* [17]

> *Everyone who believes that Jesus is the Christ has been born of God, and everyone who loves the Father loves whoever has been born of him... Whoever believes in the Son of God has the testimony in himself. Whoever does not believe God has made him a liar, because he has not believed in the testimony that God has borne concerning his Son. And this is the testimony, that God gave us eternal life, and this life is in his Son. Whoever has the Son has life; whoever does not have the Son of God does not have life.* [18]

The lyrics of *Knowing You, Jesus* sum it up well:

> Knowing You, Jesus;
> Knowing You, there is no greater thing;
> You're my all, You're the best;

You're my joy, my righteousness;
And I love You, Lord

---

[1] Proverbs 9:10

[2] Tyndale House Publishers. (2015). *Holy Bible: New Living Translation* (Ge 2:22–23). Tyndale House Publishers.

[3] Isaiah 11:2-3a

[4] Isaiah 55:8-9

[5] Romans 11:33

[6] Zephaniah 2:3

[7] Isaiah 33:6

[8] Matthew 5:6

[9] Tyndale House Publishers. (2015). *Holy Bible: New Living Translation* (Ps 5:3). Tyndale House Publishers.

[10] Psalm 119:105

[11] Exodus 6:6-7

[12] Psalm 34:4-6

[13] Exodus 14:18

[14] Matthew 9:4-6

[15] Romans 1:18-20

[16] Ezekiel 6:9b-10

[17] 2 Corinthians 6:2

[18] 1 John 5:1, 10-12

Chapter Eleven:
Encountering Stillness

In 2003, my friend and I visited the Chapel of the Holy Cross in Sedona, Arizona. After seeing the architectural wonder we browsed through the gift shop, and a small desk ornament caught my eye, and my heart. Made of Jerusalem stone, it is inscribed with *"Be still and know that I am God. Psalm 46:10"*; and it still rests on my desk today where I notice it every time I sit down. It seemed so important that I buy it at the time, but little did I realize the impact those few little words would come to have on my life now, twenty years later.

A new season of pondering stillness began for me around the first of March, 2020. Reading a Christian novel, my attention was caught by one sentence, "The solitude highlighted his ability to hear beyond the wind, beyond his own thoughts, and accept the truth."[1] At the time I had no clue that I'd be writing about stillness, but I wrote in my journal, "What a great way to express, 'Be still and know that I am God'".

Three weeks went by and again from my journal:

> Pondering how to, "Be still and know that I am God." I get stillness as I sit quietly in His presence, reading/studying/writing/praying, but I want the stillness 24/7. Lord, please plant Your stillness deep within me so that I cannot be shaken.

Two or three more weeks passed, and I was feeling as if my quiet times with the Lord had become stale. Yes, I'd been reading my Bible, praying and writing in my journal, but why did the spark of the Holy Spirit breathing new life and insight into a passage seem to have diminished? But then or, more correctly, but God! One day, as I was complaining to Him yet again, I had a definite sense that I needed to stop working so hard to study and learn and just get back to the simple truth of just being still and knowing that He is God.

The very next day, I saw a prophetic word by Lana Vawser that confirmed in detail exactly the same things I was sensing from the Lord. A short portion is shared below:

> I heard the Lord speak again: **"Do not lose the stillness. Cultivate the stillness, for treasures in stillness await you.** Do not rush ahead; do not run ahead."
>
> It is imperative in this hour to be surrendered in stillness to His way, His agenda, His pace, His timing and His direction. There is a weighty and beautiful sacredness in what is being poured out right now, which is to be stewarded with an open hand, a stillness of heart, to allow Him to have His way—whatever that looks like...waiting on Him for as long as it takes for Him to speak, reveal, lead and direct. His glory is increasing and will continue to increase as we wait upon Him in the stillness... [2]

Then a friend sent me something that Jim Goll had written about Psalm 46:10:[3]

> The word 'know' is not the word for information, it's a word of intimacy. So, to be invited into a realm of knowing God in the level that God knows us requires a precondition—be still.
>
> That's not easy for a lot of us. It's like a snow globe—you know, those ornaments with scenes

you can shake, and the snow goes all around. It is busy. But then you set it down and all the chaos settles and comes into place, and there is a beautiful scene.

That is often the way our lives are.

One time the Holy Spirit spoke a phrase to me and said, "Quietness is the incubation bed of revelation."

That set me on a journey of learning how to quiet my soul before God.

We are the temple of the living God. And just like the temple of the Old Testament, there's an outer court, an inner court, and a most holy place. There is a lot more noise in the outer court, less noise in the inner court, and there is no noise in most holy place at all.

Clearly, no one person holds a patent on God's truth, but it is always such a blessing when He seems to be speaking to multiple people in the same season with similar messages, all of which conform to His written words throughout the Bible. Sometimes when I hear him speaking to me, it's such a huge blessing to read or hear that someone else has been getting the same thing; and this happened time and again during my journey into stillness.

At 1:05 AM about a week later, I repeatedly heard very clearly, "Abide in Me," and wrote it down so I wouldn't forget hours later when I was awake and alert. Daylight had come when I awoke again, and I had a sense that the Lord wanted me to be very still; so I told my husband not to talk to me unless absolutely necessary and went in another room where I huddled under my prayer shawl and waited. It didn't take long before I began hearing an old hymn in my mind:

> Be still, my soul; the Lord is on thy side;
>
> Bear patiently the cross of grief or pain;
>
> Leave to thy God to order and provide;
>
> In ev'ry change be faithful will remain.
>
> Be still, my soul: thy best, thy heavenly friend
>
> Through thorny way leads to a joyful end.

From my journal:

> I sense the words, 'perfect stillness' and think of a beautiful pond, of still water; and still waters run deep, unruffled by the wind/storms.
>
> Is stillness a place? A dimension that, perhaps, intersects with the rest?
>
> My sense, in the rest there is no worry - only faith and perfect peace; stillness and rest.
>
> > *He makes me lie down in green pastures. He leads me beside still waters.* [4] *(Hebrew means 'beside waters of rest.)*
>
> I ask, "In stillness, what?
>
> He answers, "A knowing, the Spirit of Knowledge.
>
> > *For the LORD gives wisdom; from his mouth come knowledge and understanding; ... for wisdom will come into your heart, and knowledge will be pleasant to your soul.*[5]

Is this where words of knowledge originate? Is this a dimension of the Holy Spirit? I sense that this stillness seems to go beyond just being quiet and still, not moving; and in this stillness there is a knowledge that I cannot be moved out of the love of God. This is the knowing aspect of stillness.

Be still, and know that I am God.[6]

If still waters run deep, is this a place in the righteous deep? What does stillness sound like? Immediately think and hear the tune, *"The Sound of Silence."* My sense is that this is a place where communication is non-verbal; a place where you find rest for your soul; and the sound of silence is God speaking within my heart. It's a knowing, not only words of knowledge but the I-just-know kind of knowledge that can't be explained; it's a place of certainty of God's truth

For everything there is a season, and a time for every matter under heaven ... a time to keep silence, and a time to speak [7]

I ask the Lord to speak to me and He responds, "Hear My heart; feel My heart (I felt love); touch My heart (I sensed compassion); follow My heart (which is doing only what the Father is doing)

The silence in Heaven that's mentioned in Revelation seems important; in that silence it seems that there is awestruck wonder, astonishment. I ask again, what is the sound of silence? And I hear, "My voice."

When the Lamb opened the seventh seal, there was silence in heaven for about half an hour.[8]

I began hearing the lyrics from *Coming Back to the Heart of Worship*, "...when all is stripped away." Is stillness a place where all is stripped away so Your voice can be heard? I have the thought that I need to research and hear, "Study, study, study to show yourself approved"; and stillness seems to be a place where the knowledge of God is overwhelming; it's not head knowledge, but knowing Him, an awareness of Him, an intimate relationship that seems to be in His deep, which feels right because that is the place of intimacy with God.

My sense that stillness resides in the Holy Place:

> *Now the point in what we are saying is this: we have such a high priest, one who is seated at the right hand of the throne of the Majesty in heaven, a minister in the holy places, in the true tent that the Lord set up, not man.*[9]

> *But the LORD is in his holy temple; let all the earth keep silence before him.*[10]

Stillness also seems to be tied to the Tree of Life (as opposed to the Tree of Knowledge of Good and Evil).

Thinking of the relationship of stillness to rest, I receive the word, "Deeper, deeper, deeper; go deeper. Deep into My heart. I live in your heart; now come and live in Mine. You've heard, 'In my house are many mansions; now come and enter into the mansion of stillness where the quiet is absolute aside from My voice.'"

"How do I get there?"

"There is a place of quiet rest, near to the heart of God"

This place of stillness is tied to waiting to hear His voice:

> *Be still before the LORD and wait patiently for him; fret not yourself over the one who prospers in his way, over the man who carries out evil devices!*[11]

So what did the Lord mean about a mansion of stillness? It was a comment worthy of more investigation, especially since 'mansion' doesn't necessarily fit our usual perception of a palatial home. Notice the difference between John 14:2 in two different versions:

> *In My Father's house are many mansions; if it were not so, I would have told you. I go to prepare a place for you.* NKJV

> *In my Father's house are many rooms. If it were not so, would I have told you that I go to prepare a place for you?* ESV

The Greek word *monai* was rendered in the Vulgate by the Latin *mansiones*, which came down through the Tyndale version to the KJV as "mansions." The use of the word "mansions" here is unfortunate because it has become infused into popular Christian culture so that one can hear some Christians speaking about the fact that they have "a mansion just over the hilltop"... The word is derived from the Greek verb *menein*, "to remain," and *monai* means "dwelling" or "abiding" places. So if the *monai* are in God's house, the NIV's "rooms," or perhaps "apartments" or "flats," would be much closer to the meaning of the text here.[12]

So what if the 'mansions' the Lord referred to are actually rooms, waiting rooms, where one can wait quietly before the Lord? Makes sense to me, and I love the idea that such private rooms are available for all who choose to come into His presence for private audiences with the King.

Within a week, the Lord had more to say after I'd waited in silence for thirty minutes or more, longing to hear from Him, but He was silent. Finally, I heard:

> In stillness, you cannot be shaken; therefore, I cannot be shaken from abiding in your heart.

Now that insight was worth the wait, especially coupled with the fact that He will shake all that can be shaken.

> *I have set the LORD always before me; because he is at my right hand, I shall not be shaken.*[13]

> *He alone is my rock and my salvation, my fortress; I shall not be greatly shaken. How long will all of you attack a man to batter him, like a leaning wall, a tottering fence? They only plan to thrust him down from his high position. They take pleasure in falsehood. They bless with their mouths, but inwardly they curse. Selah For God alone, O my soul, wait in silence, for my hope is from him. He only is my rock and my salvation, my fortress; I shall not be shaken.*[14]

If you've even been in a strong earthquake, you have a taste of how frightening it can be when the earth moves under your feet. If not, you've most likely seen horrifying media coverage of places that have been absolutely devastated by earthquakes. Add in the damage wrought by tornados, volcanic eruptions, hurricanes and all manner of other natural disasters. Then multiply the worst scenario you can imagine by at least ten, and a picture of the wrath of God being poured out on the world might begin to emerge:

> *Therefore I will make the heavens tremble, and the earth will be shaken out of its place, at the wrath of the LORD of hosts in the day of his fierce anger.*[15]
>
> *This phrase, "Yet once more," indicates the removal of things that are shaken — that is, things that have been made — in order that the things that cannot be shaken may remain. Therefore let us be grateful for receiving a kingdom that cannot be shaken, and thus let us offer to God acceptable worship, with reverence and awe, for our God is a consuming fire.*[16]

Now, contrast that wrath with the absolute stillness of God, that place where we can dwell in perfect peace and be at rest. I would think the better choice would be crystal clear.

---

[1] *Acts of Faith* by Davis Bunn and Janette Oke

[2] www.elijahlist.com/words/display_word.html?ID=29106

[3] https://godencounters.com/be-still/

[4] Psalm 23:2

[5] Proverbs 2: 6, 10

[6] Psalm 46:10a

[7] Ecclesiastes 3:1, 7b

[8] Revelation 8:1

[9] Hebrews 8:1-2

[10] Habakkuk 2:20

[11] Psalm 37

[12] Borchert, G. L. (2002). *John 12–21* (Vol. 25B, pp. 103–104). Broadman & Holman Publishers.

[13] Psalm 16:8

[14] Psalm 62:2-6

[15] Isaiah 13:13

[16] Hebrews 12:27-29

Chapter Twelve:
Stillness Absolutes

One day, during the exploratory journey into stillness that the Lord has been orchestrating, I received a long word from the Lord:

There is a call to stillness

A call going out throughout the land

A call to come near

It's an invitation for all who will receive it

Stillness is a place of absolutes; the absolutes of Yahweh, of I AM:

- Absolute rest
- Absolute peace:
- Absolute trust
- Absolute knowing
- Absolute awareness of Me
- Absolute honor
- Absolute shekinah
- Absolute completeness
- Absolute sovereignty
- Absolute quiet
- Absolute presence
- Absolute communion
- Absolute readiness (a place of preparation)

Be still, be still, be still and know that I am God

Be still, be still, be still and know that I am God

Be still, be still, be still and know that I am God

It's a recipe for relationship with Me

Remember My still small voice, *"Go out and stand on the mount before the* Lord.*" And behold, the* Lord *passed by, and a great and strong wind tore the mountains and broke in pieces the rocks before the* Lord, *but the* Lord *was not in the wind. And after the wind an earthquake, but the* Lord *was not in the earthquake. And after the earthquake a fire, but the* Lord *was not in the fire. And after the fire the sound of a low whisper.*[1]

As Jesus was not the conquering king they expected the first time He came, neither am I like anyone could ever expect. I cannot be pigeon-holed.

But in the place of stillness you will know Me; you will know My heart within your heart. You will know that you know, with certainty; and much that you know will not be able to be expressed in words for I cannot be explained. These are the mysteries for which you've longed and prayed to understand.

This intimacy in the stillness of My heart shall be personalized for all who choose to meet Me here, and they will hold secret knowledge, secret awareness of Me that cannot be spoken. It's too holy and too private for words, but your hearts will encounter My heart.

Stillness is the place of true unity of man with God; true oneness, like Jesus spoke of when He prayed:

> *"I do not ask for these only, but also for those who will believe in me through their word, that they may all be one, just as you, Father, are in me, and I in you, that they also may be in us, so that the*

world may believe that you have sent me. The glory that you have given me I have given to them, that they may be one even as we are one, I in them and you in me, that they may become perfectly one, so that the world may know that you sent me and loved them even as you loved me." [2]

We all love receiving words from the Lord. For me, this one is beyond special because I usually only get a few words at a time. But, we must always test what we think we are hearing with God's written word, which validates truth and exposes deception. Notice how the scriptures verified the truth of the absolutes I heard.

Absolute rest:

Come to me, all who labor and are heavy laden, and I will give you rest. [3]

Absolute peace:

You will keep him in perfect peace, Whose mind is stayed on You, Because he trusts in You. [4]

And the peace of God, which surpasses all understanding, will guard your hearts and your minds in Christ Jesus. [5]

Absolute trust:

Trust in the LORD forever, For the LORD GOD is an everlasting rock. [6]

And those who know your name put their trust in you, for you, O LORD, have not forsaken those who seek you. [7]

Absolute knowing:

And this is eternal life, that they know you, the only true God, and Jesus Christ whom you have sent.[8]

...that I may know him and the power of his resurrection, and may share his sufferings, becoming like him in his death...[9]

Absolute awareness of Me:

Where shall I go from your Spirit? Or where shall I flee from your presence? If I ascend to heaven, you are there! If I make my bed in Sheol, you are there! If I take the wings of the morning and dwell in the uttermost parts of the sea, even there your hand shall lead me, and your right hand shall hold me.[10]

Absolute honor:

You who fear the LORD, praise him! All you offspring of Jacob, glorify him, and stand in awe of him, all you offspring of Israel![11]

The one who offers thanksgiving as his sacrifice glorifies me; to one who orders his way rightly I will show the salvation of God![12]

Absolute shekinah (the glory of God):

And an angel of the Lord appeared to them, and the glory of the Lord shone around them, and they were filled with great fear.[13]

And the Word became flesh and dwelt among us, and we have seen his glory, glory as of the only Son from the Father, full of grace and truth.[14]

Absolute completeness:

All things were made through him, and without him was not any thing made that was made.[15]

For in him the whole fullness of deity dwells bodily, and you have been filled in him, who is the head of all rule and authority. [16]

Absolute sovereignty:

He is the image of the invisible God, the firstborn of all creation. For by him all things were created, in heaven and on earth, visible and invisible, whether thrones or dominions or rulers or authorities – all things were created through him and for him. And he is before all things, and in him all things hold together. And he is the head of the body, the church. He is the beginning, the firstborn from the dead, that in everything he might be preeminent. For in him all the fullness of God was pleased to dwell, and through him to reconcile to himself all things, whether on earth or in heaven, making peace by the blood of his cross.[17]

Absolute quiet:

The LORD your God is in your midst, a mighty one who will save; he will rejoice over you with gladness; he will quiet you by his love; he will exult over you with loud singing.[18]

Absolute Presence:

And He said, "My Presence will go with you, and I will give you rest." [19]

How precious to me are your thoughts, O God! How vast is the sum of them! If I would count them, they are more than the sand. I awake, and I am still with you.[20]

Absolute communion:

> *And I will ask the Father, and he will give you another Helper, to be with you forever, even the Spirit of truth, whom the world cannot receive, because it neither sees him nor knows him. You know him, for he dwells with you and will be in you. "I will not leave you as orphans; I will come to you. Yet a little while and the world will see me no more, but you will see me. Because I live, you also will live... If anyone loves me, he will keep my word, and my Father will love him, and we will come to him and make our home with him.*[21]

Absolute readiness (a place of preparation for us):

> *But, as it is written, "What no eye has seen, nor ear heard, nor the heart of man imagined, what God has prepared for those who love him.*[22]

> *Therefore, if anyone cleanses himself from what is dishonorable, he will be a vessel for honorable use, set apart as holy, useful to the master of the house, ready for every good work.*[23]

Also absolute is the fact that all of the absolutes that the Lord shared with me is the fact that in the storms of our lives, His stillness is accomplished by God, through Christ Jesus:

> *Then they cried to the LORD in their trouble, and he delivered them from their distress. He made the storm be still, and the waves of the sea were hushed.*[24]

> *But he was in the stern, asleep on the cushion. And they woke him and said to him, "Teacher, do you not care that we are perishing?" And he awoke and rebuked the wind and said to the sea, "Peace! Be still!" And the wind ceased, and there was a great calm.*[25]

To review, this word from the Lord began with:

> There is a call to stillness
>
> A call going out throughout the land
>
> A call to come near
>
> It's an invitation for all who will receive it

So, the question is, whom among us will respond to His invitation? There is much to gain and nothing to lose in His promises.

---

[1] 1 Kings 19:11-12
[2] John 17:20-23
[3] Matthew 11:28
[4] Isaiah 26:3
[5] Philippians 4:7
[6] Isaiah 26:4
[7] Psalm 9:10
[8] John 17:3
[9] Philippians 3:10a
[10] Psalm 139:7-10
[11] Psalm 22:23
[12] Psalm 50:23
[13] Luke 2:9
[14] John 1:14
[15] John 1:3
[16] Colossians 2:9-10
[17] Colossians 1:15-20
[18] Zephaniah 3:17
[19] Exodus 33:14

[20] Psalm 139:17-18
[21] John 14:16-18, 23
[22] 1 Corinthians 2:9
[23] 2 Timothy 2:21
[24] Psalm 107:28-29
[25] Mark 4:38b-39

Chapter Thirteen:
HOLINESS AND THE EXPLOSIVE POWER OF GOD'S HEART

Our friend, Briana Lassiter, has had much to do with this book. You may recall it was her prophetic word with which we began. Briana is among our 'abundance of counselors' wherein there is safety; and she routinely double-checks what she is hearing with us so she will not err. Early on, I had a sense to ask if she had a prophetic word; but before I could do that she texted to say she'd emailed a couple of words for me to discern, especially one that she felt clueless about. Within minutes, I called her back because that word was given to her for this book the very day that I was about to ask her if she had something! That's God, and that's unity within His Body. Briana's contributions will again become obvious in this chapter.

While pondering how to complete this book, I came across a dream from a couple of years ago in which it seemed as if I had been trying to finish a book, and each chapter may have also been a room. Hmmm, this was sounding a bit familiar, given all that has been written thus far regarding rooms. The book wasn't a biography, but it seemed as if I had lived each chapter, which again had a familiar ring to it. Most of it had been completed; but some blank pages were left, apparently for two remaining chapters that were yet to be written. Throughout the dream, I was trying to figure out all of the details that go into organizing a new book, including formatting, naming chapters, determining whether or not to include appendices, etc.

I woke up, looked at the clock and saw that it was 8 AM. I'd had a full 8 hours of sleep and was about to get up, but the next thing I knew it was about an hour later and I'd been dreaming again. There were several scenes, but the last one seemed important:

> I saw a closet that seemed to be in my home, but it was more like one that my Mom used to have. It had been emptied out, and looked as if maybe it should be painted before putting anything inside, because it was kind of scuffed. At the very least, I would clean it because around the baseboard it looked pretty dirty. But then I realized there was a small portion of the wall down there that was exposed, but it was old wood, not drywall.
>
> At some point, I saw the word 'explosive' on the back wall of the closet, but the letters quickly disintegrated and disappeared. Then, I saw the word 'repressive', which also disintegrated immediately.

Needless to say, at the time of the dream in 2021, I had questions to ask the Lord:

- What was all that stuff about a book and two new chapters to write?
- What did I need to know about 'explosive' and 'repressive'?
- Why did I see an empty closet that needed to be cleaned and painted, and had exposed wood?

Everything seemed important, but the Lord apparently wasn't in a question-answering mood that day. So I re-visited my questions the next day and while a few things became clearer, others remained a mystery:

- There was zero insight into the book
- A closet is a place where things are hidden away out of sight, and/or a place where Jesus said to hide away and pray; but this closet, while empty with nothing hidden, had the small area of exposed wood
- What of 'explosive'? Reading in John about the Holy Spirit coming as our Helper, my prayer became, and remains, for the presence and power of the Spirit to explode in my life
- And, what of the opposite word, 'repressive'? I wondered if that closet represented a place in me that had been repressed and was now cleaned out and waiting to be filled with the explosive work of the Spirit

I wasn't satisfied that I had a full interpretation but, like dreams often do, this one faded quickly and was forgotten. Until now, that is, for in the midst of the Lord speaking about stillness, it became very relevant.

One morning, while waiting on the Lord in His stillness and pondering the heart of God, I had a thought:

> It seems that the heart of God is at the core of the Triune God, like the core of a nuclear power plant perhaps. I looked that up in order to be certain of my understanding about the importance of the core:
>
>> A nuclear reactor core is the portion of a nuclear reactor containing the nuclear fuel components where the nuclear reactions take place and the heat is generated. The nucleus is a central or essential part around which other parts are gathered or grouped; a core.

> The Spirit of the Lord indwells the core of my being, and is definitely THE essential part of me!
>
> At the core of Unity among Father, Son and Holy Spirit, the explosive power is far greater than any nuclear site; it would be an explosive magnitude of power beyond anything ever seen, or even perceived, by man. It is the Power by which all of creation happened; the Power that raised Jesus from the grave; a Power that mankind can never duplicate. It's also the Power of His love, which Jesus manifested toward us when He went to the Cross and died; and it's the Power of His resurrection.
>
> To an extent, this seems obvious; but my sense is there is something much bigger here that I need to understand, and it seems related to stillness. Why?

I remembered a recent conversation with Briana in which 'explosive' came up, but couldn't recall the context, so I emailed my old dream and current thoughts to her, and she responded, "Do you remember what the Lord said to my friend in that word I had? WOW!!! I looked back at the word for him, and it's all about the Father's heart!" A portion is shared here:

> My son, seek Me and the fame that is found in My heart, for I have transitioned thee and positioned thee for intimacy. No longer will you feel like a stranger outside the gate, for you will begin to feel the love of the Father that is found in My heart as you seek Me .For you have not been fathered before, and you do not know what this looks like; for the road you have been down has been divergent from My plan…

Will you agree now to follow MY plan? For the things that concern Me are of greater importance than the things that concern thee. I want your heart; I want your faith; I want your trust and intimacy. The gifts will <u>explode</u> in thee as you walk and agree with Me…For it is My might that I am building in thee, and it is <u>My power</u> that is coming upon thee, for you can do nothing by yourself, it is all found in My heart…

The next day, I awoke at 8:30 from what seemed to be a false dream and felt alert. Instead of getting up, I closed my eyes again to seek the stillness and immediately fell asleep and entered into another dream:

Something was going on in conjunction with Briana; and then I was on the phone with Paul, trying to relate what had happened with her (I don't know if I could recall what it was, or not).

Then it seems as if I was in another place or dimension while talking to Paul, where I was getting short phrases and telling him what I heard. Then there would be a long pause, with him quietly waiting and saying nothing; and I kept getting more phrases and repeating them.

Then I was seeing two persons, one of whom seemed to be the Lord and the other was someone who was involved with communication. All the while, I was describing everything to Paul. Then I said that something was happening between the two others; and had the thought that the man, who seemed like Jesus, was Melchizedek; and He was either reaching out or giving something to the second person.

I awoke suddenly in a twilight place where I was trying to process the whole thing with my eyes still closed. I knew I'd been in a very holy place, probably the Holy of Holies; and I was trying to recall the words I'd received and shared with Paul as well as whatever Briana and I had been doing because I wanted to write it all down, but it was gone.

Finally, fully awake, I looked at the clock and saw that it was now 9:30; all that had happened had taken exactly one hour.

Only in the final edit did I realized that both this dream and the closet dream from two years ago happened after I was wide awake and then suddenly fell asleep to dream again. Since I no longer believe in coincidences, but 'God-incidences', I can only repeat Paul's oft-spoken words, "You just can't make this stuff up!"

After getting up, I entered into a time of waiting; thinking and/or praying, but suddenly everything was wiped from my memory and it felt like I was jerked up to a higher place. I didn't know if it was a good or bad lifting away and started to ask the Lord, but my phone rang and it was Paul, so I briefly shared all that had just happened before he had to get to work. During our short conversation, Briana had tried to call me so I immediately called her back and things continued from there. First she shared some of the things she'd been pondering about experiencing the Father's heart; then we began to explore the idea of Stillness being a place within the Holy of Holies:

I wondered if Stillness is located within the Heart of God; so we asked, "Is the Holy of Holies located in Stillness or vice versa?" Our immediate sense is that it is one of the rooms in

His heart and she got the NKJV verse, *In My Father's house are many mansions*, completely unaware that the Lord had whispered the same thing to me just a few days before. Our sense was that Stillness is a place within the heart of God, and it's very, very deep in His righteous Deep; in the place of intimacy with Him. Our conversation reveals how we continued to explore the subject:

> (Bri) I wonder if the Heart of God is in the height, width, length and depth.

> (Barb) That resonates with me because of my earlier sense of being rapidly pulled up into a higher place. But, I also think it may be likely that since God is omnipresent, the height, width, length and depth exist in Him.

I was reminded of some other things, and that my dream was somehow being echoed in reverse. In the dream, I went from an un-recalled interaction with Briana to conversation with Paul. Then in the physical, there was an actual conversation with Paul followed by one with Briana. She continued:

> I see a wheel within a wheel, and we are suddenly moving very quickly; going very fast, at the speed of light. I hear the Voice of Many Waters, and sense many righteous beings.
>
> I get a word, "Do not be afraid. I have brought thee into their midst this day to be a witness of a reckoning that will occur on behalf of my people."
>
> Now I hear angelic tongues, and the Voice of Many Waters is starting to speak again. "Listen my children, for the war has already been won. This is

your inheritance, the inheritance of the Son. Although you will be called to the battle, and although it may be hot and fierce, I need you to remember that the victory has already been decreed from before the foundation of the world, and from before that."

It seemed as if we were witnesses to that decree in company with all of the other beings there, and our pre-existing spirits may have actually been there at the time it was spoken, before we came here. Even before we left that place, Briana started feeling deliverance and heard, "Doubt has left." Then she sensed that an elder had a hand on her head and was blessing her. Meanwhile, she was both hearing the word 'mandate' over and over, and discerning the power of the Father's heart confirmed our experience with scripture:

> *"At that time, declares the LORD, I will be the God of all the clans of Israel, and they shall be my people." Thus says the LORD: "The people who survived the sword found grace in the wilderness; when Israel sought for rest, the LORD appeared to him from far away. I have loved you with an everlasting love; therefore I have continued my faithfulness to you."* [1]

> *And he will turn the hearts of fathers to their children and the hearts of children to their fathers, lest I come and strike the land with a decree of utter destruction.* [2]

Next, Briana discerned a sensation of pressure on her chest, comparable to what it feels to experience 5G force. It was a sensation she'd been feeling in the Father's heart before our conversation. I had sense that our mandate had both been received in that place we'd been taken, and probably agreed to it before we came here. Unlike Briana, I didn't sense the speed of traveling, but while we were there felt a sense of awestruck wonder that seemed to encompass His majesty and the Fear of the Lord. It was powerful!

In retrospect, my sense is that all that happened on the phone call with Briana, brought to light all that we had experienced together in my dream, the memory of which had disappeared.

The next morning while taking communion, I heard *Holy, Holy, Holy* playing in my mind, and realized it was the first time I'd heard or thought of it in a long time. In His stillness, I began to ponder the correlation between stillness and holiness and without a doubt, I knew that stillness and holiness go hand in hand:

> *Behold, you delight in truth in the inward being, and you teach me wisdom in the secret heart.*[3]

God is so holy that to touch the Ark was an immediate Old Testament death sentence.

> *And when they came to the threshing floor of Nacon, Uzzah put out his hand to the ark of God and took hold of it, for the oxen stumbled. And the anger of the* LORD *was kindled against Uzzah, and God struck him down there because of his error, and he died there beside the ark of God.*[4]

Yet, how do we treat Him today, now that the personal, touchable Jesus has come and walked the earth? Though ascended to the Father, He is still a man who is very approachable; and through Him we have the Spirit dwelling within and direct access to the Father who is waiting for us to embrace Him as Abba, Papa.

> *The Lord is not slow to fulfill his promise as some count slowness, but is patient toward you, not wishing that any should perish, but that all should reach repentance.*[5]
>
> *Come to me, all who labor and are heavy laden, and I will give you rest. Take my yoke upon you, and learn from me, for I am gentle and lowly in heart, and you will find rest for your souls. For my yoke is easy, and my burden is light.*[6]

I fear we diminish His holiness in our minds, in our hearts, all-too often forgetting who He is and take Him for granted. In his presence, we ought to be trembling with the fear of the Lord; not afraid of Him but awestruck with the wonder of His power, His might, His supremacy, His holiness.

I think of how millions bow down before popes, referring to them as 'Your Holiness'; but no man, whether pope, priest, pastor, layman, missionary or everyday Christian doing good works, is holy on his or her own. Man has no merit, no goodness in him aside from for Jesus:

> *God, who saved us and called us to a holy calling, not because of our works but because of his own purpose and grace, which he gave us in Christ Jesus before the ages began, and which now has been manifested through the appearing of our Savior Christ Jesus, who abolished death and brought life and immortality to light through the gospel.*[7]
>
> *But you are a chosen race, a royal priesthood, a holy nation, a people for his own possession, that you may proclaim the excellencies of him who called you out of darkness into his marvelous light.*[8]

The Lord interrupted my thoughts as I heard:

> Eye has not seen nor ear heard the treasures laid up. Neither have any ever seen the magnitude of My holiness, for such would be an instant death sentence.

I asked, "What of Daniel and John, Lord, when they saw You in their visions? Immediately, I felt the fear of the Lord with His response:

> Do you think my holiness can be contained in their few chapters? They knew only in part; yet Daniel lay abed for two weeks, and John required the assistance of an angel to stand on his feet. I say again, no man can see me in the fullness of my glory and live. You cannot even imagine My holiness! Yet, My name is routinely slandered by mankind.

> But I am gracious and merciful, so I have delayed until the fullness of My time has come. Soon; very, very soon, all mankind will see the coming of My Son. All mankind will see and cry out, "Holy, holy, holy is the Son of God." Soon, every tongue will confess My name, and it will never again be slandered. DO NOT TAKE ME FOR GRANTED!

> Enter into my house for thanksgiving and My courts with praise, for the time is short.

I asked, "Father, how does this discussion of your holiness fit into stillness? 'Be still and know' resonates over and over, but what do You want me to understand?"

> In the stillness, you may glimpse My holiness; and the deeper you go into the depths of My heart, the greater will be your appreciation of My holiness. Try Me and see; for there are still greater adventures,

mysteries, encounters for you now in this life than you have ever known. Dive deep into the stillness of My heart and prepare to be amazed. Those who encountered Me, men such as Abraham, Moses, Daniel and John, did so because of focus. Their lives were focused on me and they encountered me through the corrective lenses of My Spirit. Set your eyes on things above.

My desire for you, for my people who are called by My name, is to truly know Me; not to just talk about My holiness, but to experience it, to live in it. Expand the way you think of Me; enter into to My stillness and you will bask in my holiness in a manner which you have never known. Not just head-knowledge, but experiential knowledge - *yada*.

Wow - nothing else need be added; His *rhema*[9] word was crystal clear!

Another morning, Briana called, having awakened thinking about lovingkindness and mercy; and remembering our previous conversation regarding 'explosive' and her sense of the 5G feeling Power from the Father's heart. Our conversation continued about Stillness and Holy of Holies:

> Bri: I wonder if it is located in the Heart of God. Is the Holy of Holies located in Stillness, or vice versa? Is it one of the rooms in His heart, a mansion? (She referred to the Luke 14:2 passage, not knowing I'd had the same reference and thought a few days ago.)

> Barb: Stillness seems to be a place within the Heart of God, among many rooms (mansions), and very

deep; it's in the righteous deep where intimacy occurs.

Bri: Is the Heart of God in the height, width, length and depth?

Barb: That resonates with me to a degree because of my sense of being rapidly pulled up into a higher place. But I think it's more likely that since God is omnipresent, the height, width, length and depth exist in Him, for they are created dimensions.

Bri: I see a wheel within a wheel, and we are suddenly moving very quickly; going very fast, at the speed of light, and I hear the voice of many waters and sense the presence of many righteous beings. Also, a word:

> Do not be afraid. I have brought thee into their midst this day to be a witness of a reckoning that will occur on behalf of my people .
>
> (I'm hearing angelic tongues, and the voice of many waters is starting to speak again.)
>
> Listen my children, for the war has already been won. This is your inheritance, the inheritance of the Son. Although you will be called to the battle, and although it may be hot and fierce, I need you to remember that the victory has already been decreed from before the foundation of the world, and from before that.
>
> (It seemed as if we were witnesses to that decree; and that our pre-existing spirits may

have actually been there to witness it at a time before we came here.)

Bri: I felt a deliverance begin before we left that place, heard that doubt has left; and also sensed that an elder had a hand on my head and was blessing me. I heard the word 'mandate' over and over, and discerned the power of the Father's heart to draw or to turn, and the scriptures that validate that for me are:

> *At that time, declares the* LORD, *I will be the God of all the clans of Israel, and they shall be my people." Thus says the* LORD: *"The people who survived the sword found grace in the wilderness; when Israel sought for rest, the* LORD *appeared to him from far away. I have loved you with an everlasting love; therefore I have continued my faithfulness to you.*[10]

> *And he will turn the hearts of fathers to their children and the hearts of children to their fathers, lest I come and strike the land with a decree of utter destruction.*[11]

I had the sense that we'd received our mandate while we were there, and may have agreed to it before we came to earth. Unlike Briana, I didn't sense the speed of traveling, but while we were there I had a sense of awestruck wonder over His majesty and the Fear of the Lord was intense. The whole episode was powerful.

But God wasn't finished regarding His heart yet, and one week later, Briana texted the following insights:

> In stillness and the heart of God, the center of all three (Father, Son **and** Holy Spirit) is the only place

> where the fullness of the gifts can be expressed. It's wild because there, all of the gifts at once in may be expressed together, all working together! In one ministry time today, I was all the things at once; prophet, ruler, exhorter, mercy, giver etc. If I go only in one heart (Father, Son **or** Holy Spirit), then only one of my gifts at a time gets expressed really fully!

I responded:

> In the heart of God the perfect oneness/unity of the Lord is expressed fully. It gives new meaning to the verse that a three-fold cord is not easily broken.

Briana:

> It's very tender and sacred. You can stall out if you only stay in one heart, but in all three there is a force that pushes you through completion.

The Lord continued to speak to me about the explosive power that resides in His heart, and I had the sense to look up a closed system, which is a natural physical system that doesn't allow transfer of matter in or out of the system, although in the contexts of physics, chemistry, engineering, etc., the transfer of energy (e.g. as work or heat) is allowed. So, it would seem that in a spiritual context, He is in me, I am in Him and nothing can pull me out of His hand/heart; yet, 'energy' better described as His power can be felt by others. Then I heard Him whisper:

> I'm there; I'm always there. What you feel or perceive has nothing to do with whether or not I am there; for I am; and I will never be separated from you.

The loving power emanating from God's heart is documented in scripture:

> *And the angel answered her, "The Holy Spirit will come upon you, and the power of the Most High will overshadow you; therefore the child to be born will be called holy – the Son of God.*[12]

> *...concerning his Son, who was descended from David according to the flesh and was declared to be the Son of God in power according to the Spirit of holiness by his resurrection from the dead, Jesus Christ our Lord...*[13]

> *May the God of hope fill you with all joy and peace in believing, so that by the power of the Holy Spirit you may abound in hope.*[14]

> *For he was crucified in weakness, but lives by the power of God. For we also are weak in him, but in dealing with you we will live with him by the power of God.*[15]

We are clearly living in the last days, the time of which the prophet Joel prophesied:

> *And it shall come to pass afterward, that I will pour out my Spirit on all flesh; your sons and your daughters shall prophesy, your old men shall dream dreams, and your young men shall see visions.*[16]

Yet, even before the Spirit is poured out on all flesh, Christians already have access to the explosive power of God that comes straight from His heart:

> *For the word of the cross is folly to those who are perishing, but to us who are being saved it is the power of God.*[17]

For the kingdom of God does not consist in talk but in power.[18]

God gave us a spirit not of fear but of power and love and self-control.[19]

---

[1] Jeremiah 3:1-3

[2] Malachi 4:6

[3] Psalm 51:6

[4] 2 Samuel 6:6-7

[5] 2 Peter 3:9

[6] Matthew 11:28-30

[7] 2 Timothy 1"9-10

[8] 1 Peter 2:9

[9] *Rhema* (ῥῆμα in Greek) literally means an "utterance" or "thing said" in Greek. It is a word that signifies the action of utterance.

[10] Jeremiah 3:1-3

[11] Malachi 4:6

[12] Luke 1:35

[13] Romans 1:3-4

[14] Romans 15:13

[15] 2 Corinthians 13:4

[16] Joel 2:28

[17] 1 Corinthians 1:18

[18] 1 Corinthians 4:20

[19] 2 Timothy 1:7

CONCLUSION

We began with Paul's message in which he frequently said, "But nobody ever told me what the Christian Life is really like." No, they didn't, did they? None of us are ever given sufficient warning of how difficult it is; but our lack of knowledge is not an excuse to settle for the ideology that is so common among many Christians, "Get saved because when we all get to heaven everything will be wonderful." The Kingdom of Heaven on Earth is available **now**, not just in the 'sweet by and by' because we abide in Christ Jesus:

> *Yet he is actually not far from each one of us, for ""'In him we live and move and have our being'; as even some of your own poets have said, "For we are indeed his offspring."* [1]

It's doubtful that any of us actually enjoy persevering, waiting, enduring, counting the cost of discipleship and dying to all we hold dear; but oh, how worth the price when we learn to experience His Rest and Stillness where the cares of the world fade away.

The Apostle Paul summed it up nicely, and we end with a promise:

> *But we have renounced disgraceful, underhanded ways. We refuse to practice cunning or to tamper with God's word, but by the open statement of the truth we would commend ourselves to everyone's conscience in the sight of God... We are afflicted in every way, but not crushed; perplexed, but not driven to despair; persecuted, but not forsaken; struck down, but not destroyed; always carrying in the body the death of Jesus, so that the life of Jesus may also be manifested in our bodies... So we do*

not lose heart. Though our outer self is wasting away, our inner self is being renewed day by day. For this light momentary affliction is preparing for us an eternal weight of glory beyond all comparison, as we look not to the things that are seen but to the things that are unseen. For the things that are seen are transient, but the things that are unseen are eternal.[2]

---

[1] Acts 17:27b-28:

[2] 2 Corinthians 4:2,8-10,16-18

Printed in Great Britain
by Amazon